LEWIS E. LOSONCY is Associate Professor of Psychology at Reading Area Community College in Pennsylvania and is currently acting chairperson of the Behavioral Science Division, supervising students of child development, social work, mental health, and special education. He is a traveling lecturer in the areas of encouragement and motivation.

TURNING PEOPLE ON

How to Be an Encouraging Person

Lewis E. Losoncy

A SPECTRUM BOOK

PRENTICE-HALL, INC., *Englewood Cliffs, New Jersey 07632*

Library of Congress Cataloging in Publication Data

LOSONCY, LEWIS E
   Turning people on.

   (A Spectrum Book)
   Bibliography: p.
   Includes index.
   I. Helping behavior. I. Title.
BF637.H4L67   158'.2   77-4686
ISBN 0-13-933242-1
ISBN 0-13-933234-0 pbk.

To my family, my friends, my relatives, my students at RACC, my teachers

A Spectrum Book

19 18 17 16 15 14 13

Printed in the United States of America

Prentice-Hall International, Inc., *London*
Prentice-Hall of Australia Pty. Limited, *Sydney*
Prentice-Hall of Canada, Ltd., *Toronto*
Prentice-Hall of India Private Limited, *New Delhi*
Prentice-Hall of Japan, Inc., *Tokyo*
Prentice-Hall of Southeast Asia Pte. Ltd., *Singapore*
Whitehall Books Limited, *Wellington, New Zealand*

Contents

PART TWO:
THE TURNING-ON PROCESS

3

4

5

6

TURNING
PEOPLE ON

Foreword

Turning People On: How to Be an Encouraging Person, is a timely and thought-provoking book. In an era in which we have learned to turn on through alcohol, drugs, and sexual excesses, a creative alternative is suggested—encouragement.

Encouragement is the basic change agent in Adlerian psychology. Alfred Adler, one of the giants in the formulation of psychiatry with Freud, considered encouragement to be an essential therapeutic procedure. Adlerian writings have emphasized the significance of encouragement in facilitating professional growth.

It is fitting that Prentice-Hall, publisher of the still popular *Encouraging Children to Learn: The Encouragement Process* by Don Dinkmeyer and Rudolf Dreikurs, has chosen to offer *Turning People On* at the time of the twenty-fifth anniversary of the American Society of Adlerian Psychology, a Society that considers encouragement to be the basic component of any human change process.

Robert White, a well-known personality theorist, has indicated that encouragement is the essential ingredient of any therapeutic process that is efficacious. Regardless of the psychological theory set forth, encouragement is the factor that brings change.

The author has systematically introduced the reader to the process of discouragement, clarifying the behaviors and attitudes that constrict human growth. Shyness, acting-out behavior, neuroses, psychoses, alcoholism, drug addiction, and criminal behavior are all indicators of discouragement. We will all see ourselves in these pages as the subtle process of discouragement is explored.

The art of encouragement section presents the fundamentals of encouragement in a programmed, instructional format. The six main phases of the turning-on process include: (1) creating the ideal encouraging relationship; (2) what to look for in the discouraged person; (3) facilitating decision-making; (4) encouraging action; (5) encouraging evaluation of the action taken by the person; (6) self-encouragement.

In a world in which we are all more able to discourage than encourage, this book offers the answer not only to turning others on, but also to turning yourself on. As one focuses on finding strengths in others, one's own feeling of value and worth is increased. By extending ourselves to others, we stimulate our feeling of community and cooperation. This social interest, as first described by Alfred Adler and detailed by Rudolf Dreikurs, stimulates our own courage. The book can implement the concepts of the Encouragement Laboratory and Natural High as developed by Walter O'Connell.

The book makes the reader aware of a social skill that is of great value in one's work, in family relationships and parenting, and in all social relationships.

It is encouraging to see a young author carry forth the concepts set forth by Adler, Dreikurs, and their students. It is satisfying and rewarding to know the help that can be derived for self and others from this important contribution to the self-help literature. More important, the book illustrates that by encouraging others, manifesting social interest, one's self-esteem and feelings of adequacy are increased.

This book will redirect the reader to the seminal contributions of Adlerian literature.

Dr. Don Dinkmeyer

Preface

We live in an age filled with anxiety, depression, loneliness, and sometimes overwhelming pressure. *Turning People On* takes a thoughtful look at the most significant counteracting force to these problems. That force is *you* as an encouraging person. This book gives you a step-by-step understanding of how to develop your potential as a "motivator" to those around you. People who are unhappy, unfulfilled, anxious, and suffering from feelings of alienation and depression are not able to function as responsible, involved human beings. They feel a sense of worthlessness, and their very misery in this condition often prevents them from finding a way out of the joyless trap they are in. As a result, they become literally "turned off" in relation to their own responsibilities as members of society. They are profoundly discouraged.

In this book we talk about ways *you* can encourage such people to become useful, happy human beings—and the beautiful part of this process is that you as the encourager are benefited as well as the person you are helping. We pre-

sent a simple approach to turning people on that is adaptable
to many problems and circumstances. It is an approach that
can be used by anyone—a tool for such varied people as
parents, teachers, social workers, supervisors, those involved
in volunteer work; it can help people who are facing emotional and/or physical problems, older people who are coping
inadequately with the changing world around them, persons
whose circumstances have prevented them from getting the
jobs they would like, those with addiction problems, children
who respond to the pressures of the adult world in a way that
is destructive to themselves and to others, and even those
who simply want to be better and happier people. In short, it
is an approach that *you* can use in everyday life to enhance
the meaning and beauty of human existence for others as
well as for yourself.

In the book are ideas and theories that are presented
simply and clearly; and alongside these concepts are illustra-
tive examples from real life. In addition, there are many
exercises that will help you to easily integrate these principles
of encouragement into your interactions with discouraged
people. We will discuss the reasons why people become discouraged; symptoms that indicate that people are "turned
off"; and specific ways of dealing with those whose problems
and negative self-concepts are preventing them from living
fully and responsibly. The question that this book asks is not
"Who is to *blame* for that person's problems?" but rather
"What is the *goal* or *meaning* of that person's behavior?" It is
knowledge and understanding of goals and behavior that
enables us as encouragers to help an individual reach those
goals by helping him/her to develop more responsible actions. The blaming approach rarely works.

The message of this book isn't limited to such people as
parents with "problem children" or the families of alcoholics;
nor is it meant to be used by professional conselors alone. Its
value is that the ideas expressed within can enable *you* to be

one of those people who can take that extra effort to help discouraged, turned-off people become responsible for changing their own lives for the better—to stand up on their own two feet, and even then to turn around and give the same encouragement to others. Turn on—help yourself to accent those encouraging qualities within you to improve your relationships.

For further information about getting a "Turning People On" workshop conducted by Dr. Lew Losoncy in your home-town please write: Lew Losoncy, % Prentice-Hall, Inc.

Acknowledgments

Most of the people I have known have made a contribution to *Turning People On*. Consequently, it is impossible to thank everyone who deserves credit. I am grateful to my parents, who enriched me with their constant encouragement and support; my brother, Ron, who showed me by example the importance of going after the things you believe in; and Fr. James Ferry, a counselor, who took the time to tell a failing high school junior that he had the ability to go to college.

Professionally, thanks are in order to Dr. Don Dinkmeyer for his critical evaluations of this developing manuscript and to Dr. Richard Hess (Millersville State College), who truly understood the concept and importance of a "second chance." My deep appreciation goes to Edward Swoyer, Dr. Robert Gill, George Vogel, George Perovich, Dan Purcell, Henry Kirn, Tom Lenich, and Ivan Torres for their role in the thought-provoking midnight discussions at the Pub. I am grateful to Dr. Carl Pettinato, Dr. Robert Mellon, and Dr. Ed Silverman for their help and support to a "rookie counselor." Special thanks are due to the faculty, particularly Dr. John Mierzwa, Dr. William Stafford, Dr. Andrew Edmiston, Dr. Stephen Stillman, and Dr. Artis Palmo, at the "personalized" school at Lehigh University who gave unsparingly of the most important interpersonal element, time. I also thank Dr. Charles Zastrow (University of Wisconsin) and Dr. Vincent P. Ward (University of Connecticut) for their informative and encouraging reviews.

It is a pleasure to be able to acknowledge my gratitude to Lynne Lumsden, Mary Allen, and Norma Karlin for their consideration, acumen, and assistance in the preparation of this book. My appreciation extends to Gust Zogas, Dick Cahn, Allan Howland, Bill Smith, Harlan Douglas, Mike Weisberger, and Joe Richter for their support; to Dave Weisberger for telling his story for the readers of this book; to George Mason for his unlimited willingness to help during crises; and especially to Gene Wilkins, who, despite college vice-presidential responsibilities, had the time to complete the illustrations in this book; to Carol Storm, for her outstanding editing and typing skills; and to the "helpers" at RACC, especially Bill Baer, Jan Peoples, Cindy Rhoades, Sandi Turner, Aileen Larish, and Evelyn Morrison.

Finally, it must be mentioned that the energies to write *Turning People On* would not have been available without the rich experiences I had in learning from each of my students. I have found from them that there is never a point in a person's life when it is "too late." Our role as encouragers is to make an effort to provide the optimal conditions to create this possibility. From those seeds, the mission of this book emerged.

Prologue

DO YOU KNOW THESE FOUR "TURNED-OFF" PEOPLE?

DARRYL. "Things had better go my way or else!"
Barely four feet tall, 7-year-old Darryl has his whole household, neighborhood, and first-grade class in a constant state of attack alert. He is always fighting when things don't go his way and at times even appears to lack control of himself. His parents, neighbors, and teachers have tried everything with Darryl and nothing seems to work. He is unable to take criticism of any kind, and is avoided by his peers because of his rages.

Darryl's turned-off signs—*rebellious, destructive behavior, need to control things and people.*

RITA. "My life is a real bore, but I won't change it."
Rita, age 42, is in a rut. Every day appears to be the same for her. Rita spends most of her time smoking, drinking coffee, and watching one soap opera after another. She feels constantly

1

tired, has all kinds of aches and pains. It's almost impossible to get her motivated to do anything outside of her house.

Rita's turned-off signs—*lack of confidence, feelings of worthlessness, fear of challenging situations.*

> **JANE.** *"Please pity me—I'm so weak and helpless and you're so strong!"*
> *Jane, at 12, is the youngest child in the Thomas family. She has been constantly cared for by many well-intentioned helpers in her family, and never seems to have developed the ability to stand on her own feet. She is dependent on others and rarely finishes her homework or any other project that she starts unless she is helped by someone else. Her parents are really concerned about her ability to survive in the world.*

Jane's turned-off sign—*avoidance of responsibility.*

> **LEE.** *"If your idea was any good, don't you think I would have thought of it already?"*
> *Lee, 38, is an "expert." He knows all the right answers, and woe to the person who dares to disagree with him. His closed-mindedness on any issue is similar to that of the television character Archie Bunker. Lee is in a supervisory position at work and will not tolerate any suggestions from those under him. At home, his family is forced to comply with the inflexible rules that he sets. People around him are both angry and frightened.*

Lee's turned-off signs—*closed-mindedness, need to control others, fear of showing weakness.*

You probably know many people like these—individuals who have developed inadequate ways of dealing with life. Such people are unwilling to take direct responsibility for what they do and their rebellion, boredom, poor self-concept, and closed-mindedness not only alienates them from others but also succeeds in making them depressed, disheartened, and profoundly discouraged. In using negative coping mechanisms to achieve their goals they actually perpetuate their own "turned-off" state You, in turn, may respond to them with anger, criticism, or continuous giving in. And most likely you've found such responses ineffective in changing their attitudes or actions. *Turning People On* is a book offering you a dynamic and positive approach to helping the discouraged individual. One of its major points is to encourage you, the reader, to get to know something about the *reasons* why turned-off/discouraged people act in the particular ways they do.

Darryl, for example, seems to be saying via his actions that the only way he can be recognized is to be aggressive and hostile. He feels so inferior that he literally *fights* to "prove" his adequacy. Any time things don't go his way it enhances his deepest fear—that he is weak. The mask he wears is exactly the opposite of the real person. His goal is to make others think he is strong, and he is unable, because of his beliefs about himself, to accept the responsibility of assuming blame for any wrong actions. In addition to his violent behavior, he has become skilled at constantly shifting the blame for his errors onto someone or something else.

I failed that test because the teacher asked stupid questions.
I missed that baseball because the sun was in my eyes.
I hit Sally because she's always trying to get in my way.

People like Darryl may be willing to defend themselves in any way to avoid the possibility of seeming powerless, as is exhibited in Darryl's constant fighting.

Rita has chosen to look at life this way: "I'd rather stay home than go out there in that wild, uncertain, unkind world. It's so safe and predictable here. By staying home, I'm in charge, and I never have to face any new experiences. So I don't have to fear doing anything wrong. Of course, I'm often depressed and miserable, and the world is probably passing me by, but I don't care—I'd really rather be here."

When a person like this eventually faces "what's out there," it can be traumatic. Then the conflict is intensified. We might hear the following kinds of "copout" when Rita is forced to make the decision between going out or remaining safely stagnated at home:

> I'm really feeling ill. I'd like to go to the party, but I knew I'll get sick and spoil everyone's good time.
> I'm not going to PTA tonight—what on earth could *I* contribute?
> I'd join the Bike Club, but I'd run out of energy before I got to the end of the street!

Jane operates out of the idea that if she expresses her lack of confidence and plays the "poor me" game, people will show sympathy to her. This way she won't have to face demands that people her age face. "So, I'm different from everyone else, and am less of a person. But this isn't so bad. After all, if I can't do my homework, someone will do it for me. I really *do* need help. And besides, if I'm weak, no one will fight me." In effect, this kind of person keeps all the fringe benefits of being a young child. There's always someone who is willing to take on her responsibilities.

> I *can't* give that report for the Girl Scout meeting. My voice is so weak no one would hear me. Besides, I've had such a bad cold I haven't had any chance to look up the information.
> Oh, do you think I've got a fever? Mom said it was my turn to take out the garbage, but I guess I'd better stay inside, hadn't I?

Lee, at first glance, seems to be a confident person, one who knows clearly where he is going, what is right and wrong. Yet underneath this mask of determination and superiority is a person who doubts himself. And because he doubts himself, every interaction with others represents a potential threat to him. When someone questions one of Lee's opinions, he becomes angry immediately, using his position or force to control the outcome. He will not bend on any issue, seeing everything in black or white. This rigidity makes him obsolete in today's changing world. His domineering attitude is a result of his attempt to convince others that he is sure of himself, a definite, strong, disciplined person. But his uncertainty is all too evident in comments like the following:

> I didn't *ask* for your opinion—no son of mine is ever going to wear his hair long!
> When I tell you to do something I mean *do* it! One word out of you and you're fired!
> Get this and get it good—he's the wrong guy to be foreman—and I know what I'm talking about!

These four examples represent just a few ways people have of dodging the experience of living a full life with all the responsibilities that entails. Are they to be blamed for this? Absolutely not! How do we know we wouldn't act the same way in the same situation? And what constructive purpose does blaming *really* achieve? One of the most important things we can learn is that blaming discouraged people only serves to intensify their feelings of inadequacy. As a matter of fact, blaming was probably the reason many of them became discouraged in the first place.

What is the problem, then? Why are these individuals, and many others like them, *discouraged people*? How have they developed their turned-off lifestyle? Certainly their parents didn't wake up one morning and say, "We're going to have to nip that kid's ego in the bud, and the best way to do that is for us to be discouragers!" It's more subtle than that. Frequently those who discourage others are discouraged people themselves. What is the feeling of a discouraged person?

Did you ever have an idea that excited you and motivated you onward—then, when you enthusiastically presented it to someone else, have that person tell you point-blank that it was not a worthwhile idea? Your purpose, or the reason for you, at that moment, to exist was taken away. This very idea gave meaning to your life and someone else's failure or unwillingness to recognize this created for you a heart-stopping disappointment. The wind was knocked out of your sails. *Someone turned you off.*

The essential thing for the encouraging person to believe is that finding one's purpose in life is all-important. This is the fuel that generates whatever abilities a person has. Without this energy, even a genius would be sterile. The encouraging person must believe, as well, that people must *decide for themselves* their purposes and goals in life, but that their thinking and decision-making is facilitated when done in a relationship with an *encouraging person*.

If you know any discouraged people and would like to help them help themselves to experience life more fully, to be happier people, you may find this book interesting and challenging reading. Along the way, you'll also find yourself being rewarded. It is exciting and worthwhile to see people maximize their possibilities and assertively enjoy all that the world has to offer. It is a beautiful life experience to turn people on through encouragement.

PART ONE

THE TURNING-OFF PROCESS

Chapter 1

The Discouraged Person: Symptoms

What is it that identifies a person as discouraged? What kinds of things tell us that someone is not fulfilling his potential? In this chapter we will take a look at the major symptoms of what we refer to as "turned-off" people. Some of these are readily apparent; others manifest themselves in more subtle ways. A person's expression of his/her unhappiness can take many forms; to be able to get a clear picture of the discouraged person we must be able to spot the symptoms.

Discouraged people want what other people want —attention, recognition, self-confidence, and success in life. However, discouraged people employ ineffective ways of reaching these goals. They make use of faulty techniques because they know of no other way to reach their goals. For example, people who feel ignored may become "loud-mouths" to get attention. What they don't realize is that this very behavior leads to further rejection. So they get louder and the cycle continues. The louder they get, the more they are rejected, and the more rejected they feel the louder they become.

Such ineffective approaches have developed because "turned-off" people haven't been rewarded for more appropriate ways of gaining their goals. They have grown up in a discouraging atmosphere. No individual would act in self-defeating ways if he or she were encouraged to learn to act in ways more likely to lead to goal achievement.

SIGNS OF THE DISCOURAGED PERSON

Before you can help discouraged people, you should be able to recognize them. The number of signs is endless, but in this chapter we will examine the following major symptoms of discouragement:

Excessive need for attention
Need for power and control
Need for revenge
Dishonesty
Need for perfection
Closed-mindedness
Avoidance of competition
Avoidance of responsibility
Lack of confidence
Thoughts of worthlessness

It is important to know that these signs do not necessarily appear independent of one another. Often several of them are present, and they cause and abet still other discouraged behaviors. For instance, as we will see, the perfectionist, motivated by feelings of worthlessness, becomes obsessed with performance and success in seeking to enhance his sense of value as a person. Because he uses ineffective modes of achieving the goal of feeling good about himself, he decreases his chances of success, perhaps eventually avoiding any competition, even withdrawing from challenging (read "threatening") social situations. Discouragement, then, is like a dragon devouring its own tail in the attempt to fulfill its hunger.

Excessive Need for Attention

Seven-year-old Mark jumped up on his teacher's desk, roared, and pulled his pants down. The teacher responded by rushing, almost hysterical, to the guidance counselor. The students screamed and laughed. This reaction, giving Mark a weapon, caused him to assume "control" with similar behavior on subsequent occasions. After several conferences with the counselor, the teacher adopted a new approach. When Mark tried his "gimmick" again, she calmly said, "Mark, it's cold in here; pull your pants up." After that she was careful to observe Mark and praise him publicly when he did something constructive and pleasant.

Mark required an audience. It didn't matter whether the audience booed or applauded; all that mattered was that all eyes were focused on him. He never used this device when he was alone. The audience—the group—is important to one who needs to be noticed to affirm him/herself. Observe children riding their bicycles on a playground. If one of them falls, he may look around to see if anyone has noticed; if someone has seen him, he may cry. But often, if no one is there to observe the accident, the child will simply pick himself up and move on. No audience, no show!

Terry, a 15-year-old high school dropout, frequently entertained his group by lying in the middle of the road, daring cars to run over him. He never did this unless there were people around to gasp, shriek, and react. When an uncle encouraged Terry to return to school and gave him a job in his repair shop, Terry stopped doing his "crazy kid stunt."

Again we see an example of someone trying to prove his importance by bizarre actions, and stopping such behavior when encouragement from another person rewarded more positive actions.

Rudolf Dreikurs and Lauren Gray suggest that one of the four main goals of misbehavior is the need for attention.[1] (The others are power, revenge, and disability.) Some people develop all kinds of techniques to be noticed, feeling reassured only when they are at center stage. Being a screamer, having the newest gadgets on their cars, wearing flamboyant or inappropriate clothes, or performing some kind of exhibitionistic behavior serves this purpose. Frequently, such people are successful; they may even be considered entertaining by their friends. In school there may be the "class clown," a child who goes through all sorts of antics to make people laugh and look at him or her. The reason for this particular behavior may be that the youngster hasn't been encouraged to learn to gain attention in more constructive, positive ways, such as through schoolwork, sports, or special abilities.

Attention-seekers are emotionally immature. They need constant reassurance and make excessive demands on those around them. It can be assumed that 1-year-old children need constant attention because of an inability to encourage themselves. But when they get older, they take on more responsibility. Sometimes children (and even adults) try to go back to the safe days of their infancy to rid themselves of the increasing responsibilities they face. They may use baby talk,

[1] *A New Approach to Discipline: Logical Consequences* (New York: Hawthorn Books, 1968).

crying, temper tantrums, sulking, and even bedwetting in their bid for attention. If they receive it, their immature behavior will continue. If, instead, they are rewarded for accepting increased responsibilities, they may learn more effective coping conduct.

The person who seeks attention excessively usually is in doubt of his/her own value. Thus a girl may develop a raucous laugh so that people will notice her—she reasons that if she is *noticed*, she must be worth something. If she is not, she may develop serious feelings of rejection, and this in turn may cause other symptoms, such as power-seeking or the need to control and dominate.

Teachers and parents are often ineffective in working with individuals whose need for attention results in disruptive behavior because they misunderstand the reasons for this behavior, and use punishment to try to deal with it. Punishment, however, is another form of attention and represents just what attention-seekers want. To be punished is to be noticed, and punishment can become a tool for the discouraged person.

The important thing to know about those who frantically look for ways of being noticed is that (1) this mode of coping can be prevented if the person is *encouraged* on the occasions when more positive behaviors are used; and (2) such people are extremely immature and dependent and lack the ability to encourage themselves.

Need for Power and Control

Rudolf Dreikurs suggests that if people don't receive attention for positive, routine actions, they may then enter into a power struggle to get that attention.[2] His point is that most people ignore positive everyday behaviors because they

[2]*Coping with Children's Misbehavior* (New York: Hawthorn Books, 1972).

are "assumed." A teacher, for example, may "assume" that students will do their homework and will give no recognition when they comply. It is only when youngsters *don't* do their assignments that they are "noticed." So only negative behaviors call forth recognition.

> *Felicia, 16, usually comes home on time from her dates. Her parents assume that she must and never compliment her for doing so. However, when on one occasion she comes in late, a battle ensues. Felicia now has a ready-made weapon to "get back" at her parents whenever she needs. The family has focused on* negative, *not* positives.

People with power needs are only reassured when they are in control. So they develop skills in controlling others. Youngsters may find that crying will help them achieve their ends or gain "control" in the family. (Even adults may retain regressive behaviors to gain control.) Lee, in our Prologue, used bullying force and a "know-it-all" attitude to gain power. Using sex to achieve power and control is a common game. People who constantly use such methods do so because they feel inadequate or inferior. They are, in effect, saying that they must have their way—but they can't get it unless they use maladaptive behaviors. They operate on the idea that "Unless I'm in control, I'm worthless" and "When I'm boss, I'm important." But if the situation is one in which the power-seeker *can't* win, a phenomenon that Dinkmeyer and McKay refer to as "defiant compliance"[3] may result. This is where the "underdog" seeking power totally complies, but not in a way the "authority" would like. The following are two examples of this response:

> *After being tongue-lashed by his superior officer, Private*

[3]Don Dinkmeyer and Gary McKay, *Parent's Handbook: Systematic Training for Effective Parenting* (Circle Pines, Minn.: American Guidance Service, 1976).

Harris salutes in a very defiant way while saying, "Thank you, Sir." He is complying with regulations, but his tone and facial expression plainly denote resentment and sarcasm.

Tommy's mother tells him to pick up his socks or else! Tommy, taking her directions literally, picks them up and holds them in the air, an insolent smile on his face. Since mother hasn't said anything about putting the socks in the hamper, he will infuriate her by standing there until she must issue more directions. He is being defiantly compliant.

Frequently people with a need for power and control have been pampered or spoiled in early life. They feel that the world will accord them the same treatment their parents gave them, and that they can continue to have control and act irresponsibly as they did when they were young. But the world isn't like that. Traffic lights don't turn green just because a "spoiled person" in a hurry swears or pounds the steering wheel. Weather conditions don't change just because people are inconvenienced. Consequently, spoiled people are likely to be continually frustrated in their demands to have the world operate around their needs. And again, their maladaptive behavior only serves to further discourage them and evoke more ineffective coping. Without sufficient reward for realistic, positive behavior, they continue to be turned off to their responsibilities as mature people.

Need for Revenge

Mary, at 5, had been the center of attention in her family. When her baby sister was born, Mary became jealous because of the attention focused on the younger sibling. She started to adopt attention and control tactics. Bedwetting and baby-talking sufficed in getting her temporary attention, but eventually these behaviors angered the family and no longer worked.

Then Mary began to pinch and jab the baby. This revengeful behavior reflected her temporary discouragement. When her parents saw the problem and allowed Mary to be the "big girl," and help out with her baby sister, she began to behave in more acceptable ways. She was receiving positive *attention from her family.*

Dreikurs believes that when discouraged people fail to get attention or power, the next logical step is to seek revenge.[4] It is important to remember that revengeful behavior springs from discouragement. And although it is an inappropriate way of reaching a goal, it is sometimes very effective. The revengeful person becomes the intimidator, the blackmailer, the expert on others' Achilles heels. He or she seeks out people's weaknesses and attacks. If revengeful behaviors work, they continue. Some people even maintain a complete lifestyle based on revenge. It affects their relationships with everyone; sarcasm and sadism become a way of life. Then it is easy to develop a distrust of anyone who expresses a sincere concern about them. The discouragement is so deep that these individuals feel it impossible that someone could honestly care about them. Obviously, their solution to achieving their goals is not the best for themselves *or* for others.

It is possible for people to become so preoccupied with revenge that they even recall incidents that happened years before in which they were criticized, and then devote their life to getting back. But this behavior is obviously self-destructive; moreover, it is a way of not facing the realities of daily life. It uses a tremendous amount of energy in non-productive ways. No wonder the vengeful person is discouraged and turned off!

[4]See his *Coping with Children's Misbehavior.*

Dishonesty

Imagine three reasons why people would lie—write them in below:

1. _____

2. _____

3. _____

Did any of your reasons match psychiatrist Alfred Adler's conception of lying?[5] He felt that some people who are in the habit of lying believe that there is a "heavy hand," a punisher, somewhere around them. So, one motive for lying might be *fear of telling the truth*. Children know that if they point their finger at someone else when the vase spills, they may be able to "get away with" the mistake. This is an ~~avoidance of responsibility for personal behavior because of fear~~. In an atmosphere in which truth rather than physical punishment is emphasized, a person has less pressure to lie. You can probably think of other ways you could deal positively and encouragingly with dishonesty motivated by fear.

Another motivation for lying might be *~~to appear more important in someone else's eyes~~*. A person who uses this type of deception is fearful that the truth isn't enough to make him/her recognized. People who lie for this reason are telling others that they feel unimportant. Did you use this or

[5]*Understanding Human Nature* (New York: Greenburg Publishers, 1927).

words similar to this in your list of reasons why a person might lie?

Haim Ginott suggests saving the child's face by turning his or her lie into a wish rather than a fact,[6] since frequently children's untruths reflect wishes. For example, when Brigit says, "Mom, I just saw two red giraffes on Main Street," her mother could reply, "Oh, Brigit, you mean you *wish* you saw two red giraffes on Main Street. That would be funny, wouldn't it?" Here, Brigit's self-esteem is maintained and she learns to differentiate between wishes and facts. Can you think of other ways you could deal with lying motivated by the desire for recognition?

~~Sometimes people couple lying with revenge~~. Jealous people may *slander* someone else so that others may think less of them. These people believe that the further they push someone else down, the higher they themselves go. This type of lying may exist, for example, in families in which parents react to "tattle-taling" or "telling" on others. Youngsters who tell tales then learn that enemies can be punished or viewed negatively just by the creation of a story. Many adults are a little more subtle in this approach.

> *Miss T., a social studies teacher, is unhappy in her teaching situation. She is new in town, feels she is unattractive, and has few friends. She resents the closeness of the two other teachers in her department, so she sets about to cause a split in their relationship. Taking each one of them aside, she says, "I don't see how you can stand ———, the way she talks about you behind your back." Soon the friends are separated—and Miss T. can now choose which one she will seek as her friend. But she runs the risk of having one of them find out about her dishonesty.*

Ignoring unproven claims may be the most effective

[6]*Between Parent and Child* (New York: Avon, 1965).

way of dealing with people who always seem to have something destructive to tell about others.

These examples are only three of the many motivations people have for lying. Traditionally, lies were treated with the birch rod or the heavy hand of a parent or teacher, but this only temporarily solves the problem. The dishonest person is not a sinner, but rather a person reflecting a need. You can help this person to become encouraged to fulfill the need by using more constructive behavior, and the lies will stop. But first you must seek the motive for the dishonesty.

Need for Perfection

Elinor, age 10, tried to draw a horse in art class. She was continually unsatisfied with her product, however, constantly erasing or asking for new paper. Eventually, she broke into frustrated tears. Although her teacher thought the drawing was very good, Elinor, an "A" student, wasn't happy. She missed art class for the next few weeks.

People with an overwhelming need to do everything perfectly are trying to cover all potential sources of weakness. Their greatest concern is that they may fail and look bad. Consequently, perfectionists plan every detail, sometimes for months ahead. They lose their spontaneity, and panic when something unexpected happens. They have frequently been raised to believe that they are only worthwhile when they succeed. Their parents may have been extremely concerned with performance, and their "little perfectionists" incorporated their high standards.

Perfectionists are their own worst enemies. They believe that unless they are faultless, they are worthless. And they have a very difficult time keeping up with their self-expectations. Sometimes they even deliberately set their goals low to avoid failing. Every time they are in a new situation, they become frightened about the possibility that they may make a mistake, and if they do, they relive it over and over again mentally. Need for safety, security, and predictability become predominant for these discouraged people. Even their time for "fun" is overplanned. Their attitude is, "I'm going to have fun even if it kills me!"

Another characteristic of people who are obsessed with perfection may be an inability to be in touch with their emotions. They may appear cold, logical, and mechanical—like Spock in the television series "Star Trek." But the failure to understand and be in contact with their emotions is a protection. So perfectionists frequently become "intellectualizers." Their relationships with people are on a *mechanical* level. Here is a conversation that illustrates this:

HAROLD *(age 8)*: *Mother, can I have that double dip of ice cream you promised me for doing my homework?*

MOTHER *(mechanically)*: *No, Harold. You didn't complete the homework. You only did half the assignment.*

HAROLD *(becoming mechanical)*: *Well, since I've done half, can I have a* single *dip?*

MOTHER: *No, Harold. The original agreement was based on an all-or-nothing premise. You did not fulfill the complete requirements and consequently you will receive no ice cream.*

Perfectionists tend to hide behind contracts or rules (in fact, clichés often seem to be their recipe for life). In this way they avoid personal responsibility for their lives. They seem to be saying, "I'm only following the rules that my parents, bosses, or some other authority puts forth, so don't blame me—go to them." They may panic in an unforeseen ambiguous situation in which they are forced to make a decision. People like this should not be blamed—blame is probably what caused the discouragement in the first place. Their greatest fear is personal failure, so they comply rigidly to some external standard. An understanding of the reasons for their behavior and an encouraging attitude is much more apt to be helpful to them.

Closed-Mindedness

The more discouraged people are, the greater is their need to fit the world into a comfortable black and white, right and wrong framework. They become inflexible to the demands of a specific situation and look for answers according to some previously set forth principle or law. They have a bevy of quotes and guidelines for their behavior.

Spare the rod, spoil the child.
A stitch in time saves nine.
A penny saved is a penny earned.

People who are closed-minded tend to compartmentalize everything and everyone. Upon meeting someone, they immediately love or hate that person. These opinions rarely change, even with the advent of additional information. Their view of the world and their ideas are resistant to change, even when facts are available to the contrary. They frequently speak in generalizations:

"Women are worse drivers than men."
"All Irishmen are drunkards."
"All Blacks have rhythm."
"Kids with beards are acid-heads."

Obviously they are crippling their lives with their narrow-mindedness. They want their world to be predictable—and when they force all their knowledge into stereotypes they are trying to avoid facing choices and responsibilities. Each situation has only one correct answer—theirs.

Avoidance of Competition

Some discouraged people retreat from life and its challenges. They feel safer in a confined and limited environment. They seldom go anywhere, choosing to live their lives in a safe, bounded area. They prefer a few friends who are themselves noncompetitive, supportive people. They resist any situation in which they might be placed in the limelight, choosing never to be noticed. It is not uncommon to find that people who avoid competition have been raised in a competitive family with a great deal of sibling rivalry. Perhaps their parents pitted one child against the other. Chronic losers in situations like this tend to react by becoming overly competitive, reliving their battles with everyone they meet, or by avoiding competition totally.

Discouraged people who seek to avoid competition are easily recognizable. They agree with everyone, and never engage in any controversial discussions. They try to be very sensitive to others' feelings since they feel that their very survival depends upon not stirring up any muddy water. If someone disagrees with them, their previous defeats come back into recollection. As a result, they are very difficult to know. In effect, they are social chameleons, changing their opinions for every new situation and with everyone they meet. They often find trouble, however, with this necessity to constantly shift. Sometimes they get into embarrassing situations because they have agreed privately with two people who disagree. Because no one really knows where they stand, occasionally they are criticized for their inconsistencies. This only proves to them that it is safer to stay out of social and work affairs. As you can imagine, they are seen as "push overs" and receive little respect from others.

Avoidance of Responsibility

Billy, age 9, claims he doesn't understand his homework. His "helpful" parents are more than willing to chip in some time, and usually wind up doing most of it. What they don't realize is that they are helping to develop irresponsibility in Billy. They have taught him how to avoid being accountable for his behaviors. He will not know how to cope with "days of reckoning," such as test days.

Six-year-old Susie can tie her shoes. However, she has learned that if she procrastinates and takes a long time, impatient mother will eventually do it for her. So Susie learns to play games to keep from doing unpleasant or difficult things.

People who consistently avoid responsibility for their actions are trying to protect a very unstable self-image. They may blame the teacher when they fail a test or force others to make decisions for them so they will be "off the hook" if the choice is bad. The discouraged person is extremely frightened of responsibility and develops many techniques to avoid it. Sometimes weakness if used as a way to "coerce" someone else to take on their responsibilities.

Many discouraged people are skillful, as well, in blaming others for their mistakes. As long as the blame and responsibility are shifted on to someone else, the self-image is not threatened. Such people may lean quite heavily on rules, regulations, and bosses—their feeling is that as long as they follow the guidelines perfectly, any mistakes can be credited as the result of the rules, or of those who made the rules. These people dislike making decisions or judgments. They cannot make a decision that doesn't fit into some pre-existing regulation; they become nervous, tense, and put off their decisions as long as possible. The problem with this lifestyle is that the world doesn't accommodate people who must agonize over every choice. And *not* making a choice is a choice in itself—often it is the most consequential one.

The ultimate goal of helping discouraged people is to have them come to the point of taking full responsibility for their behavior. So an encourager must be sensitive to any signs of dependency. It is sometimes gratifying to a person with a need to control others to have someone become increasingly dependent upon him. But this can be dangerous. From the beginning, helping people to "stand by themselves" must be constantly kept in mind. When you serve as a crutch, the person will never learn to walk alone. It is easy for even the well-meaning helper to fall into a trap of taking the responsibility. The pattern looks something like this:

DAVID: *I don't know what to do with myself anymore. I'm bored.*

SALLY: *Let me help you. Let's go play some basketball.*

DAVID: *Wow, you're a nice person. I like you!*

At this point in the relationship David has evoked the pity of Sally—and David is showing skill at rewarding Sally, making her feel as though she's able to pull him out of his rut. As the relationship progresses, the problems can get more serious if this dependency is allowed to grow.

DAVID: *I hate to come over to your house like this every day, and I know you're eating, but I'd like to play some basketball. None of the other kids will play. Nobody likes me but you.*

SALLY: *You know you've been over here every day and I can't possibly play basketball with you that often. I have a life of my own, you know.*

DAVID (angrily): *Just as I thought—you're like everyone else. You don't really care about me!*

Sally now may feel pretty guilty. How could she be so cruel, being David's only friend? In this case, what she has done is develop a dependency—and this is no help to David. In fact, it has made David weaker, not more responsible. ~~Encouragement does not involve *doing* for others, but rather helping them to *do for themselves*.~~ In this case Sally need not fear. David will return with an apology, and if Sally allows it, will go right through the same cycle again.

Lack of Confidence

Confident John approaches a job interview with an attitude that says, "I can do the job and your company can profit from my abilities." The potential employer feels positively about John. (S)he feels John is capable of taking on the responsibilities of the position. John is hired and this gives him even more confidence.

Bob, lacking confidence, meekly goes to a job interview with the feeling, "I'll never get this job anyway." He is apologetic throughout the interview and limits his responses to unsure yes or no answers. The employer reads Bob as a person incapable of assuming the responsibilities of the position. Bob never hears from the company again and this bears out his conviction that he is not worthwhile. His confidence is lowered and his next presentation of himself will be even poorer.

Discouraged people have lost their courage. They have lost trust in themselves and their ability to deal with others. Consequently, they don't try. If they don't make attempts, they obviously can't succeed. So another vicious cycle appears. Failure to try leads to lack of success, and this very lack of success discourages any further attempts. Once people lose confidence, their whole approach to life changes. Their facial expression, their walk, and even their goals in life come to show their negative self-image. As we all know, how a person presents her/himself is important in determining how others will perceive her/him. People lacking confidence present themselves to the world in a manner that causes others, as well, to lower their confidence in them. This, in turn, is communicated back to the discouraged people, convincing them anew that they are worthless.

Thus, people lacking confidence anticipate failure and all too often get it. They put minus signs on themselves that are obvious to the rest of the world. There are, however, some secondary gains associated with this lack of confidence. First of all, it may attract others who try to help. (Sometimes the insecure person uses this knowledge not to change, but to get attention. And in doing this he doesn't become stronger, only less responsible in his manipulations of others for his own needs.)

Dinkmeyer and Dreikurs, in looking at the social consequences of behavior, have discussed the payoffs people receive for their lack of self-confidence.[7] If it is more socially rewarding for some people to lack confidence than to be confident, obviously the former condition will prevail.

Another payoff may be that other people might assume that persons lacking confidence can't do things and will take on their responsibilities. We discussed this earlier in this section.

Sometimes people lacking confidence try to overcome feelings of inferiority by acting in the opposite manner (as we saw in the example in the Prologue). They put on a mask of superiority to cover up their weakness. They may become boastful and make up stories about themselves. At times, they give a cool, confident image and the appearance that everything is under control (see Figure 1–1). Many times these people are quite successful with this façade, but it takes a great deal of energy to keep that mask up. Their greatest

[7]Don Dinkmeyer and Rudolf Dreikurs, *Encouraging Children to Learn: The Encouragement Process* (Englewood Cliffs, N.J.: Prentice-Hall, 1963).

Figure 1–1

concern is that someone may notice their very weak point. So, the weaker or the more inadequate they feel, the thicker and heavier the mask that is needed to cover that feeling of inferiority.

>   *Tom flunked out of college in his freshman year while his friends went on to complete school. Whenever he got together with them, he prepared by reading recent magazines and even looked for "big words" in the dictionary. He tried to impress his friends with his knowledge. This took a lot of time and energy. His friends, not having these feelings of inadequacy, could be themselves. They could use their energies constructively. Tom, however, was obsessed with the feeling that he mustn't look inferior. This soon became obvious and annoying to his friends, and Tom became less sought-after.*

>   *Robert, a fourth-grader, was the class bully. Everyone was afraid of him, and avoided any contact with him. One day in a*

counseling interview Robert confided that he believed he was physically weak. His mask had been developed to cover up his most basic fear—that is, of being recognized for his physical weakness. True, everyone was afraid of him, but he used a tremendous amount of energy in maintaining this mask. It was only after a number of counseling sessions that Robert found he could let down the mask and be accepted without being a bully.

So we can see that the seriousness of people's feelings of inferiority sometimes can be inferred by the intensity of their "superiority actions." Also, those who *appear* cool and confident may well be discouraged people who will panic easily when they are challenged. However, challenging them only creates more feelings of inferiority; as is true of blame, challenging is not included in the encourager's repertoire of helping methods.

We should note here that lack of confidence is brought about by *feelings* of inferiority, not by inferiority itself. We all know people who seem to be unaware of a weakness they may have, even though everyone else notices it—so the negative point doesn't influence their behavior. Only those things that people are aware of are capable of influencing them. This is not to disregard unconscious factors as behavior determinants: rather, it suggests that most people are affected not by the way the world is, but by the way they view the world. Thus, to best understand discouraged people, it is important to see the world the way *they* see it, not the way we see it. How many times have you judged someone to be confident until you had a chance to get to know that person better and found just the opposite to be true?

Thoughts of Worthlessness

Discouraged people confuse their worth with their performance. This confusion leads to the feeling that if they are successful at something, then they are *worth more*, and if they fail they are *worth less*. That impression of worth makes their worth affected by moment-to-moment successes and failures.

Often people who feel worthless have been raised in a home in which they are accepted only when they performed well—for example, when they got good grades, excelled at a sport, etc. These people, consequently, are only able to feel worthwhile at certain times. As long as they meet the approval of others, they are acceptable. But when they have angry feelings or do something that they have learned to evaluate as not being "good," they will dislike themselves again.

It's harmful for people to evaluate themselves in terms of performance. No one can possibly succeed in everything he or she does—if self-concept is based on wins and losses, a person may eventually stop trying. Albert Ellis suggests that if people rate themselves according to some standard, it should be the standard of their "being" or "aliveness."[8] A person might say, "I am good, not because I do very well at anything and not because certain people tend to approve of me, but just because I am alive, because I exist, and because I can make choices." With this philosophy, people's worth would not be tenuous and dependent on each moment. Discouraged people cannot accept this position and frequently choose to look at themselves as having "part-time value." Anyone who appears to be unmotivated to make an effort in life may be too strongly steeped in the notion that if he tries and fails, once again he will be reminded of his own failure as a person. The encouraging person must be constantly sensitive to this possibility.

A PORTRAIT OF THE DISCOURAGED PERSON

People are not born "turned off"; this process occurs in social experiences. Adler suggested that the inevitable feel-

[8]*Humanistic Psychotherapy* (New York: McGraw-Hill, 1973).

ings of inferiority that infants have, deriving from their early dependency on others, causes them to exhibit a "striving for superiority" and a desire to "master" their world.[9] Through interaction with others, they soon realize that there are unsafe and threatening aspects of that world. If these environmental experiences overwhelm their desire for independence, they may become discouraged, and either of two trends may develop. The first is an active preoccupation with "disproving" what they believe to be the world's judgment of them. This translates itself into behaviors aimed at achieving attention, power, or revenge; dishonesty and perfectionist tendencies are also typical of this type of discouraged person. The second trend is a passive acceptance of the world and its apparent evaluation of them. Here, the signs of discouragement may include thoughts of worthlessness, lack of confidence, avoidance of responsibility, avoidance of competition, and closed-mindedness. The specific discouraged behaviors that develop are dependent upon "what works" for people in their social environment, as well as what specific factors have led to the negative view. If people find that the best way they can disprove the world's harsh judgment of them is through dishonesty, for example, then this is the pattern that emerges. Once specific signs of discouragement develop, they will continue unless it becomes rewarding for them to act in more responsible ways. When the payoff system for discouraged people changes and they are rewarded and encouraged to be more positive and responsible and mature, the "turned-off"behaviors no longer serve a purpose and are no longer effective.

The discouraged person is acting in the best way he or she sees to achieve individual goals. Often, however, ways chosen to attain these goals can be ineffective and may alien-

---

[9]*Understanding Human Nature* (New York: Greenburg Publishers, 1927).

ate others. Discouraged people may realize the inappropriateness of their actions, but simply not know that there are alternatives approaches. In an *encouraging atmosphere* they are more likely to "take risks" in seeking alternative solutions. (In Chapter 3 we will discuss enriching our lives through risking alternative approaches.)

Discouraged people are ego-involved rather than task-involved in dealing with life. Instead of trying to seek solutions to problems (task involvement), their goal is to look good and not appear inadequate (ego involvement). Their successes make them feel worthwhile, while their failures bring out thoughts of worthlessness. "How do I look?" may be more important to ego-involved people than *"What is the best solution to this problem?"* Every experience in life is immediately viewed from a personal standpoint. Every experience, as well, represents potential success or failure for them alone. And all too often such people spend their lives defending themselves rather than experiencing life.

Ego-Involved	*Task-Involved*
1. Must have own way.	1. Looks for the *best* way; if someone else's way is more effective, then that way is more appropriate.
2. Closed-mindedness.	2. Open-mindedness.
3. Panics when wrong.	3. Learns from errors to improve future behaviors.

Possibly the most serious consequence that discouraged people face is related to what Rosenthal and Jacobsen call a

' self-fulfilling prophecy."[10] In their words, "people, more often than not, perform according to their expectations of themselves." They go on to say that there is a relationship between a prophecy and an event. If discouraged people *expect* rejection from others, they will more likely experience it. It may be related to their lower level of self-esteem, their defensiveness, and this may become the cause for the rejection.

Related to this idea is Frieda Fromm Reichmann's theory that the psychotherapist's own belief about a patient's success might be, in an important way, the determinant of that success.[11] The implications of these thoughts is clear for the encourager—if we *expect* a discouraged person to respond positively to encouragement, perhaps he/she in turn can learn to expect positive results and behaviors of him/herself, buttressed by our help.

The ideas in this chapter suggest that it is primarily through their social relationships that people develop discouraged behavior patterns. Optimistically, then, more positive and appropriate behavior can be developed when there are *changes* in the discouraged person's social relationships. This is where the encouraging person comes in—one skilled in understanding the meaning of the discouraged person's behavior, and willing to accept that the other can only change him/herself.

Following is a table presenting an outline of how discouraged behaviors develop: their goals, the typical reaction of others; and alternate, more encouraging reactions. It will be helpful to you in understanding and dealing with discouraged people. In the next chapter we will discuss four of the major ways in which maladaptive, self-defeating people *get* that way.

[10]Robert Rosenthal and Lenore Jacobsen, *Pygmalion in the Classroom* (New York: Holt, Rinehart and Winston, 1968).

[11]*Principles of Intensive Psychotherapy* (Chicago: University of Chicago Press, 1950).

TABLE 1
Behaviors and Goals of Discouraged People

Behavior	Possible Goal of Behavior	Typical Reaction of Others	Alternate, More Encouraging Approach
*Attention-seeking	Attention. Feel important when noticed.	Reprimand. Punishment. "Giving in." Name-calling (e.g., "brat").	Ignore. Give attention for more appropriate behaviors. Leave the situation (if the audience leaves, the show ends).
Avoidance of responsibility	No pressure. No fear of failure. Safety. Predictability.	Name-calling ("lazy"). Taking responsibility for the discouraged person.	Encourage responsible behaviors. No help with responsibility.
Lack of confidence	Safety. Retreat from reality. Pity.	Sympathy. Pity. Blame.	Encourage effort. Support.
Thoughts of worthlessness	Attention. Pity. Praise-seeking.	Praise. Pity. Blame.	Show how worth isn't dependent upon performance but on existence.
Avoidance of competition	No losses. Not noticed, singled out, or put on the spot.	Giving "Special treatment."	Emphasis on trying—not winning. Communication of idea that a loss is only a suggestion that there is an alternative way of handling a problem.

Behavior and Goals of Discouraged People *(cont.)*

Behavior	Possible Goal of Behavior	Typical Reaction of Others	Alternate, More Encouraging Approach
*Need for power and control	Domination. Security-seeking in being boss. Reaction against weakness, inferiority. Get own way.	Anger. "Giving-in." Name-calling.	Ignore inappropriate behaviors. Try to give attention for cooperative behaviors. Refuse to debate.
*Seeking revenge	Attention. Retaliation. Control. Hurt.	Hurt. Giving in. Fighting. Name-calling ("no-good person").	Ignore when possible. Point out the results of revenge. Provide more desirable alternatives.
Need for perfection	Success in limited area. Predictability. Security.	Impatience. Reward for success.	Encourage risks, new experiences. Support when things don't go. well. Emphasize effort.
Dishonesty	Escape from punishment. Enhance self. Escape inferiority. Punishment of a rival.	Punishment. Name-calling. Punishing others. Blaming.	Emphasize truth, not punishment. Point out lie in supportive way. Ignore tattling.
Closed-mindedness	No confusion over values. Predictability. Avoidance of personal responsibility.	Agreement. No pressure.	Encourage new experiences. Help the discouraged person view openness with pride.

*Partially adapted from Don Dinkmeyer and Gary McKay, *Parent's Handbook: Systematic Training for Effective Parenting* (Circle Pines, Minn.: American Guidance Service, 1976).

CASES AND QUESTIONS

Exercises

Identification of Signs of Discouragement

Use your creativity, coupled with the knowledge you have gained about discouraged people in Chapter 1, to suggest some ways of helping the following discouraged people.

Helen, 35, has a great deal of anxiety for days before going to a party. She constantly thinks, "What if I don't look well?" "What if my clothes aren't in style?" in addition to many other, similar concerns. When the day of the party arrives, she prepares herself for hours. Rarely is she ever satisfied with her appearance; sometimes she even gets sick and doesn't go.

1. *What are her primary signs of discouragement? (Refer to Table 1.)*

   _____

2. *In what kinds of possible social experiences may this have developed?*

   _____

3. *What are some approaches you might use in helping Helen?*

   _____

George, 54, is going to lose his job unless he gets his high school diploma or passes the equivalency test. He quit school in the eighth grade and claims that he is too stupid to pass the test or even to take classes that will earn him a diploma. He doesn't want to even try the test, is convinced he will fail.

1. *What are his primary signs of discouragement?*

_____

2. *In what kinds of possible social experiences may this have developed?*

_____

3. *What are some approaches you might use in helping George?*

_____

   Calvin, age 7, is the son of a professional football player. Yet, during recess, when the other youngsters play football, Calvin leaves the group and usually gets into trouble. He may run out into the street dodging cars or throw stones at the other children.

1. *What are his primary signs of discouragement?*

_____

2. *In what kinds of possible social experiences may this have developed?*

_____

3. *What are some approaches you might use in helping Calvin?*

_____

   Joe and Mary M are having problems with their daughter, Megan. Megan, now 17, wants to stay out "like her friends" until 1:00 after a special dance. Mr. M angrily declares that the rule for good girls is to be home by midnight, and wants no compromise of that standard—it's either 12:00 or nothing! Mrs. M isn't sure, but separately she tells both her husband and Megan that she agrees with them. She tells Megan that even though she agrees, however, her father is the boss.

1. **What are the primary signs of discouragement of both Joe and Mary?**

   (Joe) _____

   (Mary) _____

2. **In what kinds of social experiences might these signs have developed?**

   (Joe) _____

   (Mary) _____

3. **How could you approach helping first Joe, then Mary?**

   (Joe) _____

   (Mary) _____

   Herbie, 10, is living with his divorced mother. He brags to everyone that his father is a millionaire, was an Olympic swimming champ, and now is working for the CIA, and because of the confidential nature of his job, Herbie cannot reveal to the neighborhood children where his father is. None of these claims is true.

1. **What are Herb's primary signs of discouragement?**

   _____

2. *In what kinds of social experiences may this have developed?*

_____

3. *What are some approaches you might use in helping Herbie?*

_____

   Joan and Carl, both 29, have been married for eleven years. Both are high school graduates and Joan has decided to go to college. In her first term there, she earns a B+ average. Carl has become quite depressed recently, misses work frequently, and makes self-depreciating comments such as, "Looks like someday you'll make more money than me," and "I must bore you." Joan considers the possibility of quitting school since she feels responsible for Carl's depression.

1. *What are Carl's primary signs of discouragement?*

_____

2. *In what kinds of social experiences may this have developed?*

_____

3. *What are some approaches you might use in helping Carl?*

_____

4. *What are some approaches you might use in helping Joan?*

_____

   John, 21, the youngest of six children, lives with his mother and father. Since his graduation from high school, he has been unsuccessful in his search for work and for the last year or so hasn't even bothered to try. He says, "It's no use —nobody is hiring." His parents have catered to his every whim. They don't take vacations because they fear he can't handle himself alone. They even go with him to buy his clothing. They seem to enjoy taking responsibility for John. They pity him and feel he would be incapable of succeeding by himself in the cold, cruel world.

1. *What are John's primary signs of discouragement?*

   _____

2. *In what kinds of social experiences may this have developed?*

   _____

3. *What are some approaches you might use in helping John?*

   _____

4. *What are some approaches you might use in helping John's parents?*

   _____

Questions

How Well Do You Understand Discouraged People?

1. Name some attention-getting behaviors that
   a. A child might use.
   b. A husband might use.
   c. A wife might use.

2. What is the goal of attention-seeking behavior? How might you deal with someone's excessive need for attention?

3. Why do some people do things for which they know they will be punished?

4. What are the advantages of playing the "weakling" game (e.g., I can't tie my shoes, do my homework, etc.)? What is

the best way of dealing with the weakling? What are some of the behaviors you might see in this person?

5. In what way is the perfectionist discouraged? What does the need for perfection show?

6. Distinguish ego-involved from task-involved behaviors.

7. List three reasons for dishonesty. What are some of the needs of a dishonest person? How can you best deal with these needs?

8. What is the power-seeker's greatest fear? What is the perfectionist's greatest fear? What is the attention-seeker's greatest fear?

9. What are the advantages of avoiding competition?

10. How is the revengeful person discouraged? What can be done to change his/her revengeful behaviors?

11. Explain and give an example from your everyday life of the self-fulfilling prophecy. How does it work against a discouraged person? How can it work *for* that person?

12. What is "defiant compliance"? Give an example.

Chapter 2

The Subtle Process of Discouragement

How does it happen that people give up the adventure of maximizing their possibilities, close their ears to new ideas, turn off, and come to the point of viewing life as nothing more than the process of trying to "get by" from one day to the next? In this book we suggest that such a pattern has developed from a number of discouraged social experiences. This chapter will attempt to describe ways in which the discouragement process begins—the "techniques" that are used, deliberately and unintentionally, to make a person feel discouraged and devalued. But we should add a word of caution before going on:

> At the crux of the whole discouragement process is *blame*. This may include blame of self or of others. In both cases the result is discouragement. As you read this chapter you may become more aware of times when you have discouraged others. If you choose to blame yourself for these experiences, you will be in no

position to become an effective encourager. Rather, you will "back into" encouraging others out of guilt. Guilt-motivated encouragement is both insincere and ineffective. Some of the chapter material will, as well, cause you to remember times in which other people discouraged you. You may get angry, decide to blame them, or even wish to retaliate. This is not the purpose of this book.

It is possible to learn from the experiences of the past (task involvement) to develop into a more effective encourager in the future. So, if you see yourself or others in the examples, it is healthier to search for ways of handling similar situations in the future in a more positive way rather than wasting energy feeling guilty or angry. Our impressions of the past are always inaccurate, colored by our perceptions and needs. And the past is over. You are starting this moment with a clean slate, and since you have chosen to read this book, it must be assumed that your intentions are positive. Look at it this way: *No matter how bad your golf game was yesterday, none of it is recorded on today's scorecard! You are now at the first tee.*

TECHNIQUES OF DISCOURAGEMENT

There are many, many ways of discouraging people, most of them quite subtle. Discouragement takes place every day and in many social interactions. Most discouragement is not intentionally planned, but this, of course, is of no consolation to the defeated person. Some techniques of discouragement will be mentioned here with supportive case studies. You should try to envision some other ways in which discouragement occurs. It is through further understanding of this process that you can help to affect positive changes in the lives of those around you. The techniques we will look at include:

Discouragement through domination
Discouragement through insensitivity
Discouragement through silence
Discouragement through intimidation

Discouragement through Domination

There are two major types of dominators—those who dominate through strength and those who dominate through an appeal to weakness.

Type I Dominators

Type I dominators are able to discourage people by providing their "strength" to "help" others. What they say, however, is not always what they *mean*.

Surface Message	Underlying Message
Here, let me give you a hand with that.	Let me do it; you'll mess it up.

> *Betty and Ray have recently married. Ray's mother (being a helpful mother and concerned about Ray's health) insists on showing Betty how to cook for him. She is constantly visiting their home with outstanding treats such as Beef Wellington and Lady Baltimore cake. As a result, Betty feels a great deal of anxiety every time she cooks for Ray. How could she ever match his mother's performance?*

Betty is discouraged and possibly even angry. Her mother-in-law, while trying to be helpful, has created an example that is impossible to follow. Unless Ray is very sensitive and has open communication with his wife, he may not realize the cause for the strain in the relationship between Betty and his mother. He probably does notice, however, that Betty never suggests that she'll cook dinner for his mother.

Betty's discouraged signs:

> Lack of confidence
> Feelings of worthlessness
> Avoidance of competition

> *Ms. M, a first-grade teacher, insists that the children in her class only take home superior drawings to their parents. Seven-year-old Roland has extreme difficulty drawing, but still makes an attempt. His picture of a tree, because it is inferior by Ms. M's standards, is largely redone by her before the end of the school day. She can't understand why he is fretful and fidgety as he takes "her" picture home.*

Ms. M is conveying the message to Roland that his artistic ability is inferior without her help. The picture, in actuality, is no longer Roland's production. The encouraging person recognizes a very healthy sign in the fact that Roland is still willing to try despite the teacher's implication that he lacks ability. But his unhappiness is a sign of discouraged symptoms to come. It is less likely that he will make more attempts after a number of experiences such as this. And if he stops trying altogether, there will be no improvement to encourage him.

Roland's discouraged signs (complete):

_____

_____

Type I dominators like to take on all the responsibilities. They allow people no chance to think for themselves or make their own plans. Since they assume that they alone know the right way to do things, they become impatient with others' "inferior" ways. People who have been consistently discouraged by these dominators tend to feel inadequate, incapable of making decisions, and they learn to seek out other dominators in life. They tend to become more and more dependent, and some reach the point where they cannot even perform the simplest chores without "encouragement" or help of some kind.

Type II Dominators

Not all people dominate others through strength. Type II dominators are able to assume control in quite a different way, but their control can be just as complete, and just as devastating to others. Like Type I dominators, however, their message is different from their words:

Surface Message	*Underlying Message*
Listen to me—I'll protect you.	If you grow up, I'm afraid you won't need me any more.

Ted, 19 and the last of eleven children, wanted to get his own apartment. He was earning $210 a week, but his parents felt that he was immature and couldn't make it on his own. After many threats and hassles, they finally gave their approval. Ted moved out, but during the first few months his parents called him continually to find out if he was all right. After a while, Ted concluded that they had been right, and moved back in with his parents. However, in those months he had learned a great lesson about life and the cost of living. A year later he moved again, and this time he was well-prepared *and sure of himself. His parents, seeing this, relaxed and let him live his own life.*

After trying to dominate through overprotection, Ted's parents finally took a risk. They allowed Ted the opportunity to develop some responsibilities. He achieved a better understanding of life and independence by resisting the temptation to live in the controlled, protective environment of the family home.

Carl, 17, brought his mother and father with him to his high school guidance counselor for some career explorations. The conversation went as follows:

COUNSELOR: *What are your interests, Carl?*

CARL'S FATHER: *Oh, he likes drafting and mechanical drawing.*

COUNSELOR: *Are you taking mechanical drawing here at school, Carl?*

CARL'S MOTHER: *Yes, and he's doing really well.*

COUNSELOR: *Carl, I'm asking you the questions, and your mother and father are answering them. Can you tell me why?*

CARL'S FATHER: *No, he's too shy!*

It's not likely that Carl was born shy, but rather that he developed this in the domineering social relationships he experienced. His mother and father were probably overly sensitive to his developing needs, so Carl never really *needed* to talk. They had all the right answers and provided a comfortable life for their son. The only price he had to pay was to submit to their domination. How equipped is Carl to cope with life? The encouraging person views the goal of parenting as one that helps the child become independent of the parent.

Carl's discouraged signs (complete):

Domination of any type stifles growth and helps to create people who are turned off, discouraged. Dominators tend to view people as weak and incapable of standing on their own two feet. (You can probably see by now that those who discourage by domination are often discouraged people themselves, and act to accomplish their goals in ways that are ineffective and/or inappropriate.) Clearly, it must be remembered that the goal of encouragement is to have others take on more responsibility, not less. Encouraging people see themselves as equal to and not more important than discouraged people. Encouraging people, as well, have trust and confidence in others' abilities. Although in the beginning there may be "risky" moments in allowing someone to grow, many discouraged individuals are quite capable of assuming responsibility when given the chance.

Discouragement through Insensitivity

People who discourage others through insensitivity have it in their power to inflict great damage. In many cases they may not even realize they are acting irresponsibly and causing others to "turn off." Sometimes, though, they act deliberately insensitive in order to accomplish goals of their own (revenge, closed-mindedness, dishonesty, need for power and control, etc.). Their messages, too, are mixed.

Surface Message	Underlying Message
Wait till later, honey— I don't have time to listen to your poem now.	I'm much more interested in what I'm doing than in your blasted poem.
That's really a horrible color on you, Terry.	You look great, and it threatens me.

The Rigid Steel Company has a suggestion box available to all of its workers. Joe, a 22-year employee with the company, submits an idea. Although the idea has merit, the supervisor of his department puts Joe down, saying, "If it was such a good idea, don't you think I would have thought of it years ago?" The supervisor, who feels inadequate, consciously or unconsciously fears that Joe, a bright man, may take over his job.

Apparently, this suggestion box is merely a token to give employees a feeling of involvement. Joe "took a risk" and was criticized for it. Joe's behavior was quite healthy, but the cold rejection of it made him discouraged and angry. The people in the company did not realize it, but they had a loyal person who wanted to be helpful and who felt a part of the company. Joe's anger caused him to criticize the company publicly. Frequent battles with the supervisor occurred. How differently this could have been handled with some encouragement! Don't look for many further suggestions from the employees in this department.

Joe's discouraged signs:

_____

_____

Supervisor's discouraged signs:

_____

_____

> *Mr. W, an eleventh-grade science teacher, has asked for more questions from his class. This suggestion is followed by a question from Martha. In response to Martha's question, Mr. W replies, "I just finished talking about that—where were you?" Martha, hurt and embarrassed, thinks, "I'll never talk in class again."*

Mr. W never really understands why the students don't ask questions. Although he requests more verbal participation, he sends signals to the students that are contrary to that message. Martha learns her lesson. From this point on, she'll be less likely to ask a question.

Martha's discouraged signs.

_____

_____

> *Kelly, 7, after scoring the winning touchdown in an imaginary football game with himself, comes running into his house proclaiming, "I'm going to be a football player!" His father, engrossed in the sports section of the newspaper, pats his son's head and replies, "Good, good. Now go back outside and play." Kelly's joy turns to anger.*

At this moment Kelly was saying, "I've found a purpose in life, a goal, a reason for living." He now had something to strive for, however temporary. Kelly's father forgets how he might have felt as a youth in this same situation. Kelly's joy at achievement and goal-setting are not recognized by his father—thus he thinks, "Maybe my ideas are stupid. Next time I'll keep them to myself."

Kelly's discouraged signs:

_____

_____

Observe young children when they have an idea they feel good about and want to express. Their eyes sparkle, they speak enthusiastically, their energy level increases and they aren't afraid to reveal their idea to someone else. Compare this with the attitude of senior high school students with an idea. They may take a chance and express it to the group, but the presentation will probably lack the vigor of the young child's. They may even express it in such a casual way that no one even picks up the point of their message. Now think of an adult expressing an idea. This may be done almost apologetically—in fact, rarely do adults express ideas with the zest of youth. Now ask kindergarten children how they like school. Ask senior high school students and you may get quite a different opinion.

What happens along the way to people to make them lose the naturalness, enthusiasm, and desire for growth so commonly associated with youth? Most people tend to become more afraid of being honest, of taking risks, and of even showing happiness to the full emotional extent that they feel it. In this book we suggest that people develop this more calcified trend partially as a result of insensitive social relationships.

Discouraged people, especially, tend to be unwilling to take risks. They develop a feeling that people don't really care, since they've never really been heard by others. It is crucial to understand this point. In an encouraging relationship the helper must listen to peoples' ideas *with sensitivity*. He or she aims not to repeat what has been done to the discouraged person so many times before. Negative critical evaluations of someone in the early stages of a relationship may close off any possibility of unearthing that buried youth with its sense of excitement, enthusiasm, and desire for life. The helper listens and imagines, "How would I feel if I were expressing what this person is expressing to me?"

Although the total encouragement process is discussed later in the book, it is appropriate to note here that this sensitivity and empathy are the most important ingredients in encouragement. If the helper hears comments such as, "I've never told anyone these things before," or You're the only one who understands me," the seeds to risk-taking, growth, and new life are planted.

Discouragement through Silence

The general themes of those who discourage through silence are something like this:

"Only weaklings need a pat on the back."
"If you compliment someone, you're likely to spoil him."
"A person's paycheck is the only reward he/she needs."

Carolyn worked as a nurse in a Midwestern state. She felt quite adequate about her job there, looking forward to going to work each day, and felt as though she made quite a contribution to the hospital. Some time later, she and her husband moved to another state. With her excellent references, she quickly secured another nursing position. But after three months, she resigned, saying that she felt she was no longer a competent nurse. When asked what she did differently at this hospital that made her imcompetent, she replied, "I did everything the same, except here no one ever said how I was doing, so I assumed I was performing poorly." Carolyn is undecided about her career, but she has expressed an interest in areas not related to working around people.

Supervisors frequently don't realize the motivating force behind occasional social praise. In this case, for example, they lost an effective employee. Although they may have been aware of Carolyn's superior performance, they assumed that good workers don't need recognition and praise.

Carolyn's discouraged signs:

_____

_____

Mr. V and Mr. L were team-teaching a course in psychology. While at the "Pub" after class one evening, they discussed the outstanding progress of Bill, one of their students. It occurred to them that they were telling the wrong people—they should have been telling Bill. The information discussed between them was sterile, but they saw that if they mentioned it to Bill it could become a great source of energy and motivation to him.

The point of *Turning People On* is that positive information you have about a person is meaningless unless it is communicated to that person. The school counselor who "files" information about a student's positive progress in a manila folder without communicating this to the student is placing emphasis on a task—and this is inconsistent with the principles of turning people on through encouragement.

How would you imagine Bill felt when he was told by Mr. V, "Mr. L and I have noticed how hard you've been working in psychology class"?

Silence is *not* golden in the early phases of the encouragement process. The encourager does not assume that people know that they are doing well. Failure to communicate positives may lead to discouragement in people. Consider the possibility that many people go through an entire day without any encouragement. Someone cooks meals, someone is on time for meals, someone does his or her homework, someone takes out the garbage, etc. These "roles" are frequently not acknowledged. Too often, only when people withdraw their services are they noticed. So they learn that they receive attention only for negative reasons—doing something "wrong" rather than something "right." If you can change this process for a discouraged person, you may be helping that individual take the first step to turning on to life again.

Discouragement through Intimidation

There are several types of intimidators; their ability to discourage is awesome. They, as well as those they threaten (deliberately or without the intention of harming), are in need of the principles of positive encouragement.

Type I Intimidator "I know something you don't know."

Type I intimidators may cause discouragement by relying more on cold facts than on more subtle and hard-to-get data in their interactions. Such people may discourage others with every intention of being helpful, as our next example shows.

> *Dave was failing his tenth-grade year, so his parents decided to have him tested. After the tests had been completed, the psychologist told Dave and his family that the results indicated*

that Dave didn't have the ability to go to college. He felt that he reassured Dave and his family, however, by suggesting occupations that require little education. He commented, "Dave, you could be a truck-driver—the best truck-driver in your town." Fortunately, Dave and his parents refused to accept this judgment, and they pursued the idea that the boy still had the ability he had shown in grade school. They saw another counselor—one who looked beyond present test results—and a few weeks ago, Dave returned to town after earning his B.A. from a major university, having accepted a management position in a large hotel chain. With positive encouragement and a large measure of determination, Dave overcame what could have been a lifelong pattern of discouragement through intimidation.

Statistics and testing, quite helpful in the counseling process, are not infallible instruments. A sensitive psychologist recognizes this and talks about ranges of possibilities, not a sealed fate. The individual involved in test-taking can easily be intimidated by his or her inability to understand the terminology of psychometry. The intimidator in this case looks only at numbers or scores. Frequently an individual's interests, goals, and values are overlooked, and in a sense these are the most important predictors of success.

Type II Intimidator "I'm assuming perfection from you—anything less than perfect is worthless."

Type II intimidators, too, are apt to be insensitive to the total person. For reasons of their own, they demand an unrealistic standard of perfection from those in their control.

On the first day of school the teacher tells 8-year-old Chris that she has had all of Chris' brothers and sisters in class at one time or another and that they were all "straight A" students. "I'm expecting great things of you, Chris," she says. She notices later that Chris isn't a very responsive student. In fact, as the weeks go by, her schoolwork gets more and more "substandard."

Chris has been intimidated by the possibility that she can't come up to the teacher's expectations. The family comparison has brought forth the idea that Chris has everything to lose and nothing to gain. At best, she can just do what is already assumed. And more than likely she may feel that her brothers and sisters are much brighter—thus she becomes almost paralyzed, more and more convinced that she can't measure up.

Chris' discouraged signs:

_____

_____

Type III Intimidator "Oh, that's nothing—I've got one better than that!"

These intimidators are also apt to be thoughtless and self-centered. The accomplishments of others only stir them to boast of their own actions—playing the "one-up" game.

> *Mrs. Gold experienced one of the most exciting moments of her life when her first child, Jenny, age 1, took her first step. Full of all the joy of parenthood, she proudly called her neighbor on the phone to share her ecstasy. The conversation went as follows:*

MRS. GOLD: *Guess what? Jenny took her first step!*

NEIGHBOR: *I know just how you feel—when Todd was nine months old I remember how he was able to walk and run.*

*And when JoAnn was ten months old, she was not only
walking, but could talk as well. Those kids of mine always
seemed to do everything faster than anyone else—by the
way, have I told you about Tod's being elected class presi-
dent? And JoAnn. . . .*

*Mrs. G's joy has been compromised. She has been intimi-
dated and is less likely now to call someone else to share her joy.
She thinks, "Maybe this isn't a big deal anyway."*

Intimidators are frequently manipulative and like to be
in control. Often, they lurk in the surroundings of success.
There they can set the stage to put others down. It's easy to
become discouraged in this atmosphere.

There are many types of intimidators; for example, the
"dictionary reader" who tries to impress others with vocabulary, rather than trying to communicate on an equal level.
Almost anyone's feelings of inadequacy are thoroughly acti-
vated in the presence of an intimidator. Again, such people
don't always *consciously* try to discourage others; but for their
own building up their attitudes and words serve to put other
people lower on the totem pole. Their failure to acknowledge the feelings of others can be instrumental in causing
discouragement.

SUMMARY

The process of discouraging others is usually very subtle
and unintentional. There are many "techniques" of discouragement, and in this chapter we have examined four main
types. *Discouragement through domination* is accomplished
either through strength ("I can do it better") or supposed
weakness ("I need you to need me"). In either case the purpose is to take over the responsibilities of another person.
This is exactly opposite of the encouragement process, in

which the most important thing is to help another person develop the ability to assume responsibility for his or her *own* life and actions. *Discouragement through insensitivity* occurs as a result of one person's inability or unwillingness to empathize with another. An insensitive person can be instrumental in causing another person to develop a negative self-image. Sensitivity to the needs of others and the ability to empathize are, in fact, the single most important ingredients in the encouraging process. *Discouragement through silence* is a subtle and devastating technique. One of the major points in this book is that positive information about someone is meaningless unless it is communicated, and those who are silent about others' good qualities can do as much harm as if they had deliberately set about to hurt. The final method of discouragement we discussed in this chapter is *intimidation*. Sometimes this occurs because of concern with cold facts rather than with personal considerations. Knowledge of the goals, needs, and interests of an individual are vital, but often well-meaning people concentrate on statistics, records, and percentages rather than on the human being who needs help. Another way of intimidating is to demand absolute standards of perfection. This, too, indicates a more mechanistic approach. Finally, there is the person who discourages by always one-upping others. All types of intimidation, whether deliberate or unconscious, manifest a lack of concern for the deep human needs and well-being of others.

Questions

How Well Do You Understand the "Turning-Off" Process?

1. Describe some techniques of discouraging people.
2. Think about times in your life when you were discouraged by others. In what ways might they have encouraged, rather than discouraged you?

3. Who was the most discouraging teacher you've ever had? How did this person discourage?

4. What might be some qualities of a person who continually discourages?

5. How are people who discourage through dominating discouraged themselves?

6. Reread the section on "Discouragement through Intimidation." Have you ever been intimidated in these ways? What type of needs do you think your discouragers had?

7. Have you ever discouraged through silence? Think of three people to whom you could have communicated positive feelings, but didn't. Consider your reasons for this failure.

8. Why is it ineffective to blame people who have discouraged you? Why is it unproductive to blame yourself for times in the past when you have discouraged others?

PART TWO

THE TURNING-ON PROCESS

Chapter 3

Becoming
an Encouraging Person

Now that we have seen what makes a person turn off to the world and his/her responsibilities in that world, and now that we've talked about some of the signs of discouragment people show, we can begin to deal more concretely with the process of encouragment—how we can turn people (including ourselves) on to a richer, more fulfilling life. In this chapter we will discuss the importance of perceptual alternatives[1] in developing an encouraging personal outlook in an ever-changing world. Then we will examine the problem of finding *meaning* to our lives—organizing all the perceptions into a purposeful coherent whole that allows us to function well in our world. It is important to remember that the more ways we have of "looking at" our world, the more capable we are of living and adjusting to it.

[1]Perceptual alternatives refer to the many different ways of viewing and interpreting the same situation.

OPENNESS TO CHANGE: ENRICHING YOUR PERCEPTUAL ALTERNATIVES

A basic tenet of encouragement implies that in today's rapidly changing world, one's ideas must continually be open for inspection. Stagnation is the tendency to remain the same, to always respond to problems in the same stereotyped way. Consider Archie Bunker in the television program "All In the Family." When he is confronted with a new idea, Archie immediately rejects it because he is threatened by anything that doesn't fit into his rigid ideas of the world. This keeps him restricted and limits his choices and experiences. Further, it makes him a negative and discouraging influence on those around him.

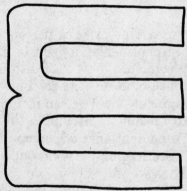

Figure 3–1

What do you see in Figure 3–1? A letter "E"? Turn your book and view it differently. Can you see a "W" or an "M"? Think of all the different perceptual alternatives or various ways of looking at the same symbol.

There are many different ways of seeing something. A football field, for example, appears quite different from an airplane than it does from the grandstand or from a position on the field. Yet it is the same field. People who are able to live a happy, responsible, "turned-on" life can view the world from many perspectives. Figure 3–2 is a diagram showing various degrees of openness. The first drawing illustrates people who spend all their energies trying to maintain sameness; such individuals are rigid and closed to new ideas. They

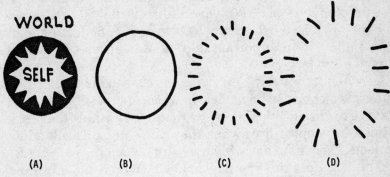

Figure 3–2

have a set, inflexible way of viewing the world. They are threatened and tie their worth into defending what they believe in. Even when new information appears, they disregard it. Whenever they encounter a new situation, they respond in the same, predictable way. They are easy to understand.

With encouragement, these "turned-off" people can move in the direction of (B) in the illustration. They can learn to accept more outside data in order to expand their perceptions. They may still, at times, respond to new situations in the old, rigid way, but *they now have alternative ways of handling problems*. They are learning to look for the truth (task involvement), rather than spending all their energy ineffectively seeking to maintain a tightly defined conception of the world (ego involvement).

After achieving success in learning to perceive more options, people can move in the direction of (C), then (D) in the illustration. The goal of the encouraging person is to help people impel themselves toward this state of being. In (D) there is total awareness at every moment; the individual can respond in many different ways to every new experience. It's almost as if the self and the world were one, as Maslow suggests in his conception of the "self-actualizing" person.[2]

The encouraging person recognizes that people's ability to develop *perceptual alternatives* is directly linked to their willingness to take a risk, to grow. Overcoming the fear of taking risks, then, is an important step *out* of a turned-off, discouraged lifestyle.

Unquestionably, everyone faces situations in which there is a choice to be made—in which one possibility represents growth and the other, stagnation. Consider the crucial times in people's lives when they face these difficult adjustments. The first day of school, for example, represents a choice, as does the first day on a job. In both situations people must leave their safe homes, where life is secure and predictable, and enter an environment that holds much threat and uncertainty for them. How easy it would be to take the "safe way" and stay at home. Yet the result would be a bigger problem the next day. Moreover, when one has chosen growth—the expansion of experience—there is the constant fear of failure. It is often easier to retreat than to go forward.

Can Perceptual Alternatives Be Developed?

Absolutely! People can move in the direction from (A) to (D), but this involves work. It involves being open to all new experiences before drawing tentative conclusions—tentative, because the encouraging person views truth as a moving river. That is, truth may be felt or experienced as a

[2]Abraham Maslow, *Motivation and Personality* (New York: Harper & Row, 1954).

result of the data currently available, but as the data change, so does truth. Positive people view the search and the process as important in themselves. They are more inclined to say, "Let's see if this works better than that in this situation" rather than, "This is definitely the answer." When people feel they know all the answers, they are thinking in a rigid, stereotyped, "turned-off" way and they have lost their ability to adapt to new data. It's important to remember that *it is in the search* that people find their meaning.

At this point perhaps it will be beneficial to try some exercises that will help you discover the ways you can develop perceptual alternatives.

> **EXERCISE 1.** *Think of the last time you were in an argument or discussion with someone. You, of course, can remember the position you took. Now, consider the other person's argument. Imagine you are that person with all of his or her experiences and his or her present knowledge and situation in life. Really empathize—try to get into his or her skin. You are searching for the* inner *reality. Now try taking that side of the argument governed by that inner reality. If you find the other person's argument more convincing and, in effect, more believable now, you are moving in the direction of achieving more* perceptual alternatives. *You have a better understanding of the other person because you've been provided with another way of viewing the world outside yourself. You also have earned a bonus—because you now have a better understanding of the other person; maybe you are a little more tolerant of him or her.*

People naturally tend to view the world from their own perspective, experiences, and socialization. The male laborer who argues that the working person is getting a raw deal may change his tune when he's promoted into management. The college student who rebels against the Establishment may in a few years own a business and alter her viewpoint. The encouraging person tries to recognize that there are as many viewpoints as there are people and arguments to defend. This person also knows that his or her position is not superior, just different. For example, consider the following questions from different perspectives:

1. Was Benedict Arnold an *American traitor* or a *British hero?*
2. Is communism a form of government *squelching individual freedom,* or is it the *fairest of all ways of governing people?*

Get the point? You may always have taken your belief system for granted. Perhaps now you can see that other belief systems are possible—that because they are different doesn't mean they are "wrong." Maybe Benedict Arnold was *both* a British hero and an American traitor. Remember how many different ways you can view a football field. The person with perceptual alternatives immediately recognizes different viewpoints. This person doesn't blame, but attempts to understand opposing points of view.

EXERCISE 2. Think about a situation in which you felt bad. It might have been failing a test or a "put-down" by someone. For example, if it was failing a test, you could view that test failure in many different ways. Some ways might include:

1. *I must study much harder for the next test.*
2. *School isn't for me. I studied as hard as I could and I didn't make it.*
3. *That stupid teacher has something against me.*
4. *I didn't put the right answers in the correct places.*

5. *I knew I'd fail. Mom and Dad were right when they told me I was taking courses that were too ambitious.*

6. *I'll learn from this. Mistakes are nothing more than suggestions that there are alternative answers or better responses.*

Which answers would you have been most likely to give?

Get the idea? In effect, you can be self-defeating by responding in a stereotyped fashion, believing that failure means you are stupid and worthless. This is unproductive. The more positive and realistic your alternatives are, the better able you are to cope.

How many different ways could you think of for explaining or dealing with your own discouraging situation? Did you find possible relief in some of your perceptual alternatives? Were there any tentative solutions in any of your perceptual alternatives? If you had trouble with this exercise, you should go back to the first exercise. If you didn't have any trouble, then you are increasing your ability to perceive events in many ways. You are becoming less rigid, more open, flexible, and more capable of living in this changing world. You are altering, as well, your inner reality.

EXERCISE 3. *Take an object at home. Stand above it and study it. Now look at it from the sides and concentrate. Pick it up, if possible.*

Consider the different ways of viewing that object. How is the object different according to the different ways you look at it? Interestingly, as you look at the object in more ways than one, you learn more and more about it. But in a sense you may also realize that you know less and less.

Ask someone else to do the same experiment with the object. Compare notes.

If you and the other person agreed on every sensation about the object, which is unlikely, ask yourself now if you have a handle on truth. If you say yes, then consider that what you are looking at is just a conglomerate of molecules. You might not have considered this alternative before. And you thought you knew what the truth was? As you can see, what is true is relative to the time and the perceiver. A loveseat would be viewed differently by an upholsterer, a carpenter, a physicist, an enamored couple, and a vacuum cleaner salesman. In each case it is the same piece of furniture, but in each case it is viewed by people according to their relationship to the object. Increasing your perceptual alternatives will give you more ways of viewing that same external reality.[3] This will as well make you more sensitive in understanding different people.

> **EXERCISE 4.** *Imagine you are your best friend looking at you. Now write a paragraph about what you see and feel about this person.*

> **EXERCISE 5.** *Imagine you are your worst enemy looking at you. Now write a paragraph on what would probably be said about you.*

Changing Perceptions through Alternative Focusing

When people view anything, they place some elements of it into the foreground, others into the background. Those items they choose to *focus* on consequently become more significant. The following exercise will help you understand this.

> **EXERCISE 6.** *Look at a picture. Try to envision what element on that picture you are giving more attention to, or are*

---

[3] We will discuss external and internal realities presently.

focusing on. *Notice that the rest of the picture has lost meaning or has been transferred into the background. Now focus on something that previously was in the background. Look at it carefully. What has happened to the part of the picture that you focused on before? Did it drift into the background? If it did, you experienced another form of perceptual alternative —focusing. Was either way right or wrong? No, they just were! No need to judge, just to experience.*

This explains how two people can "see" you quite dif-. ferently. One may view you in a positive way by focusing on your good traits, while the other sees only your negative qualities. If you are like most people, you feel more comfortable around the first than the second person. And think about the self-fulfilling prophecy. There is a very good chance that you even do better around the first person because that person is confident in you. Around the second person, you may not be as effective.

   EXERCISE 7. *Think about two people you know. Take a minute to write down some of the traits or characteristics that you feel they have:*

Traits of Person "A"   *Traits of Person "B"*

_____   _____

_____   _____

_____   _____

_____   _____

   Did you see positive or negative traits in persons "A" and "B"?
   The discouraging person is skilled at focusing on the negative qualities of people. If you find that most of the time

you tend to see negative qualities in others, it doesn't mean that they are "bad," only that you focus on aspects or qualities of theirs that are negative. It is difficult to encourage someone if all you see is negative. (See Figure 3–3.)

Figure 3–3

The encouraging person has a knack of focusing on positive qualities of a person and *expressing* it to the person. This is a very important step in encouragement.

> **EXERCISE 8.** *Consider someone you absolutely can't stand. Now take another perspective. Can you focus on some positive traits of that person? Can you force some of this person's negative traits into the background?*

If you are successful in the last exercise, welcome! You are in the process of becoming an encouraging person.

Oh yes—one more thing. Can you express these positive traits to that person? . . . Well, perhaps you can't right now, but just wait!

WHERE IN THE WORLD IS THE REAL WORLD?

We have seen the importance of being willing to change, to look at all the possibilities. The ability to make use of perceptual alternatives and take risks is what enables a person to work toward achieving a full, rich, responsible life. But in opening ourselves up to different options, how do we decide what is real, what is important and meaningful to *us*? Given two alternatives to a situation, two different people may respond in altogether different ways. Why is this?

Everyone is influenced in his or her perceptions by (1) the *external reality* (the chair) and (2) the *internal reality* (how *you* perceive the chair).

External Reality	*Internal Reality*
An overstuffed "beanbag" chair covered with green corduroy.	A great place to flop and relax after a long, hard day.

The internal reality of the chair for your friend may be quite different—she may see it as a monstrous decorating mistake, a revolting sight!

To illustrate the importance of these influences on behavior, consider this example. If you seriously believe that no one likes you, it doesn't matter whether they really do or don't, from a strict psychological point of view. Your actions will be based on the conclusions that you draw (internal influence), not on the way other people really feel (external influence).

Can you begin to understand why two different people respond to the same situation in two different ways? One person may respond to criticism by feeling miserable; another person may respond to the very same criticism by being open and accepting of it. It is the *viewpoint* (internal reality) of the criticism that is important. When an individual is able to develop perceptual alternatives, he or she has the advantage of having several possible ways of looking at a problem. This is an important thing for an encourager to know.

If different realities exist within as well as outside of our minds, how do we find meaning to the world? The answer is that we have the responsibility to look for alternative ways of viewing the reality outside ourselves and thus be able to effect a change in our reaction to it. In most cases, people do not change external reality, but instead change their *reaction* to it. In some cases, however, they are even changing external reality.

Consider a girl in a new situation—the first day of classes at school. She knows no one. She goes into class with a great deal of apprehension and starts to wonder whether people will be friendly and whether they will like her. She sits in the back of the room and gets the feeling that everyone knows everyone else. So she buries her head in a book and ignores the group. By her interpretation of the situation (people are unfriendly), she acts in a way that sends a very clear message to them (I don't want to be bothered). Hence, as she leaves class that day, the other students avoid her and her belief is reinforced—she is convinced that they don't like her. What if she had gone into the very same classroom with the viewpoint (inner reality) that even though she doesn't know these people, they will probably be pleasant and friendly. So her behavior will be outgoing and friendly. In this case they will perceive her as wanting to get to know them, because she smiles and looks interested. Because she is able to select the *best* alternative from her inner reality, she may be able to alter the external reality.

Healthy, positive people keep seeking different ways of viewing what is in the external world in order to find the most successful way for them. They take in as much information as is possible—they are open—and they still recognize that although they make mistakes, they will learn from them rather than being devastated by them.

So we can see that when someone feels that she/he has no purpose or goal or meaning in life, this is not due to the way the world *is*—it is due to their own felt discouragement. Two people in the same situation can view it differently, the one finding meaning in the experience, the other none. But one of the most crucial points in this book is that THE RESPONSIBILITY LIES SOLELY WITHIN EACH PERSON FOR FINDING MEANING IN LIFE. Turned-off people avoid this search, since it may develop into another discouraging setback. But take that same external reality of yesterday and help a person (in an encouraging relationship) to seek alternative views of it, and that person is at the starting point again—this time with a greatly improved chance of finding an effective, positive way of looking at the situation and dealing with it. This is what we're aiming at in this book—to let you see how you can turn others (and yourself) on by an encouraging, responsible attitude.

The process of being open to alternatives and taking risks can be painful. Nothing can be taken for granted—everyone must be prepared for the possibility that some of the most basic things that have previously been accepted may have alternative viewpoints. There is no end goal, but the *process* is what is important. Temporary, workable truths (the best internal reality for a particular situation) must be sought, with a realization that there are no final truths, no final answers.

You are now at the heart of this book. You are aware of some signs the discouraged person shows and how the turning-off process may have occurred. It is hoped that you are now more sensitive to the struggles and fears that such people face when they consider the possibility of breaking the shackles of their crippling but predictable past behaviors. In the next chapter we will discuss five assumptions that will be useful for encouragers to employ in dealing with people.

SUMMARY

In this chapter we have defined perceptual alternatives as different ways of seeing and interpreting the same situation. Discouraged people resist change and risk—they are afraid of disturbing the status quo and thus act in a predictable, inflexible manner, frequently seeing things in terms of right/wrong, black/white, good/bad. As encouragers, we can often help them see other possibilities for handling their problems. As perceptual alternatives become available to them, they tend to look at the world in a more positive way and act more responsibly.

External and internal reality refer to what something in the world *is* and how we see it—and the two views are often very different. The way we interpret the external reality is vital in its determination of our subsequent behavior. The meaning we assign to external realities—to life itself—is something that is highly individual; to a large extent our success in behaving like responsible, fulfilled human beings is dependent on how open we are to all the possible alternatives. No two people perceive or respond to the same thing in the same way. Those who are able to look at an external reality (a bad test grade, for example) from several different angles have a much better chance of thinking and acting responsibly—but confining one's perceptions within a negative, turned-off attitude becomes a vicious circle in that such thinking and behavior perpetuates itself. It is important for the encourager to know that the responsibility for finding meaning to life lies with each individual. We can't "give" meaning to someone else. But we can encourage others to find their own meaning by learning about the many ways external realities can be interpreted. With an increased number of ways to look at their situations in life, people are much more capable of finding appropriate solutions to their problems.

Questions

How Well Do You Understand Perceptual Alternatives and the "Real World"?

1. Consider a decision that you are currently facing. Does your choice represent growth (uncertainty, new experience), or does it represent stagnation (safety, security, and predictability)? Consider the possible alternate consequences of each choice.

2. Think of a position in some current social issue that absolutely "turns you off." See how well you can present the other side of the story.

3. What is alternative focusing? How can you make use of alternative focusing with a discouraged person?

4. Describe "inner reality." What are the two realities, and how is the way you deal with these related to broadening your perceptual alternatives?

5. Can you take on the responsibility for providing someone with the right choices in determining their life-meaning? Why or why not?

Chapter 4

The Art of Encouragement: Some Guidelines

Before we plunge into the all-important chapter on the systematic approach to turning people on, there are five basic assumptions[1] that you ought to be able to make in order to be most effective in your interactions with discouraged people. These assumptions will serve as guidelines for your behavior as an encourager.

1. Only *individuals*, not groups, are important to the encouraging person
2. The *individual* exists as a social being
3. The *individual* functions as a whole, complete person, not as a series of parts
4. The *individual* has goals, purposes, and values that motivate his or her behavior
5. The *individual* acts according to the way he or she views the world

[1]The last four assumptions are drawn from the work of Don Dinkmeyer and Rudolf Dreikurs, *Encouraging Children to Learn: The Encouragement Process* (Englewood Cliffs, N.J.: Prentice-Hall, 1963).

ASSUMPTION I: ONLY INDIVIDUALS, NOT GROUPS, ARE IMPORTANT TO THE ENCOURAGING PERSON

Toby is an overweight, unhappy child who seems always to do the wrong thing. He continually stumbles into other students, makes inappropriate comments, and gets in the way. Jackie, the ringleader of the class, has decided to "tell Toby off," so he won't bother others any more. Jackie and her compatriots discuss ways of doing this. Chris says, "Yeah, Toby's a jerk—let's knock him over a couple of times so he'll stay far away from us." Peter listens to the others, but thinks, "Gee, that would make him feel awful. But if I say so, Jackie and Chris will be mad." Paula, a quiet girl who behaves well and gets excellent grades, thinks, "I know they're going to be unfair to poor Toby, but I'd better stay out of it."

Mrs. Wilkes wants to help Toby, but she knows that issuing a command to the group to be quiet and "treat Toby right" will not be effective. She thinks, "Chris is strong and vocal, but he agrees with everything Jackie says. Peter and Paula aren't going to take a stand and defend Toby. I've got to work with these kids individually, including Toby, to get them to get along better."

Within groups, as Mrs. Wilkes know, there exists a diffusion of responsibility, and it is necessary to focus on individual needs and responses to effect a change in behavior and outlook that will be positive and lasting. It is only when an individual knows that he or she specifically is being "noticed" or "recognized" by someone else that this person can begin to become more aware of his or her own unique importance and responsibility.

Here is an example of an encouraging approach focusing on the individual.

DR. B: *What seems to be the problem, Susan?*

SUSAN'S MOTHER: *She has a headache and a sore throat.*

DR. B: *I know your mother wants to be helpful, Susan, but you're a
big girl and are perfectly capable of telling me what is wrong all
by yourself. Your mother will be so proud of you!*

In this case, the doctor is encouraging Susan to take on more
responsibility for herself. Also, the mother is being encouraged to take pride in Susan's growing independence.
Mother's fear that her child won't express her problem cor-
rectly or that she is incapable of communicating to the outside world is being relieved by the doctor, who has the pa-
tience to wait out her response.

To verify the importance of this first assumption, try
this experiment: From a group of children in your neighborhood or your class, choose a particular youngster who
you've never really noticed before. Determine that you are
going to make it a special day for this person. You are going
to give special attention to him or her. Watch what happens
to your relationship! And watch that person blossom!

The encouraging person believes that it is the uniqueness of each individual that provides the raw material of
encouragement. The importance of a person lies in his or
her differences, not in similarities to others. Consequently,
the encouraging person sees every person as an exception to
the rule. At the proper time in the relationship the encouraging person expresses this to the individual in a way that helps
that person incorporate his/her uniqueness as a source of
pride, not shame. This helps the individual to view him/
herself *positively* and *realistically*, and not to deny obvious
differences in the attempt to cope with the world.

One obvious problem emerges with Assumption I that
should be discussed at this point: *How is it possible to have the
time and energy to focus on every person as an individual?* This is a
valid question. It is possible that encouragement may not be
appropriate for some settings owing to the limitations of time
and energy. The encourager must make the decision about
whether or not there is enough time and energy available to
help individuals change their ways of coping. But it is our

thesis in this book that the use of encouragement, in the long run, saves rather than uses energy. As you read on you will find that one of the primary goals of the encourager is to help the turned-off person develop the ability to encourage him- or her*self*. When this person can say, for example, "I like my work" rather than asking, "Is my work good?" you know that he/she is learning to be positive—to take pride in internal judgments rather than being dependent upon external evaluations. This does not happen magically, but rather is the result of some kind of a "turning-on" process. In other words, with encouragement, the self-defeating person learns to take over and assume the responsibility for his/her own behavior. Moreover, once an encouraging person develops a sensitivity to the encouragement process, it becomes second nature and involves less and less energy. Encouragement becomes a product of a person's lifestyle, rather than a consciously planned systematic method.

ASSUMPTION II: THE INDIVIDUAL EXISTS AS A SOCIAL BEING

Everyone, out of his/her early dependency, has learned to need people. Some develop overwhelming dependency needs, while others rebel against these needs and strive so hard for independence that they become loners. The former situation may develop out of encouraged dependency or overindulgence, while the latter may result from rejection. But in both cases, the individuals have arrived at their way of coping within the context of their membership in society.

It should be remembered that not all isolated people are discouraged. However, if the loner has developed out of a perception of discouraging social situations, this is certainly discouragement. If, however, the loner is personally involved in task-oriented goals and still retains openmindedness to alternative perceptions, this then is a person quite capable of experiencing further growth.

The importance of knowing that people must be understood in terms of the social group (even though their *individuality* is what is important to us as encouragers) has been stated by Dinkmeyer and Dreikurs:

> Man's behavior can best be understood if it is viewed in terms of its social setting. We should not consider either man or his behavior apart from its social situation. What is appropriate for Johnny to do at home may be most inappropriate at school. It is always important to consider the entire field within which the individual is acting.[2]

From this explanation we can see why a person might be discouraged in one setting while quite motivated in another. It is crucial that an individual who decides to encourage another person recognize this.

When a person turns his back on the world, and seems to have negated the need for belongingness, this may be a sign of deep discouragement. The encourager must be prepared to help this individual re-establish trust in others. Naturally, this will take time. When someone feels so rejected by others that he/she tries to function completely alone, this is a way of saying, "You're not interested in me, therefore I won't be interested in you—who needs you anyway?" Likewise, the person who is overly dependent must be helped to achieve a sense of responsibility to others in the social setting and this requires a secure belief in him/herself.

In short, your goal is to help the self-defeating person become capable of developing and nourishing a sense of trust in himself so that he will be able to trust in others. Trust and a sense of responsibility—both in relationship to oneself and to others—go hand in hand.

[2]*Encouraging Children to Learn*, p. 8.

ASSUMPTION III: THE INDIVIDUAL FUNCTIONS AS A WHOLE, COMPLETE PERSON, NOT AS A SERIES OF PARTS

The individual is a complete person. When Frank, for example, feels nervous and worried, it affects the way he performs on a test, drives his car, interacts with others. When he is feeling well and happy, he is more confident. When he is anxious, his ability to concentrate changes, his responses may be slower, he may even feel physically ill. Psychologists may speak of an individual's grade level, IQ, aggressive responses, etc. Physicians refer to blood pressure rate, electrical discharges from the brain, body temperature, etc. But even if the complete medical, educational, and psychological statistics of a person are gathered, we still do not have an understanding of the total person. A human being must be seen as an integrated whole; changes in an aspect of that whole affect all other aspects. This is not to suggest that we disregard the importance of the "components" of an individual, but rather that we keep in mind that the total person is not merely a sum of his parts.

ASSUMPTION IV: THE INDIVIDUAL HAS GOALS, PURPOSES, AND VALUES THAT MOTIVATE HIS OR HER BEHAVIOR

Gretchen, age 8, sits wearily on her front step, elbows on her knees and hands supporting her unhappy face. She is a picture of boredom. She ponders over the waste of a day off from school with nothing to do. Passers-by note the lack of energy this girl appears to have.

Gretchen isn't physically tired. Her dejected appearance

and glum behavior indicate that she lacks only one thing—a goal for that moment. Lack of a goal creates fatigue, frustration, and boredom. With perceptual alternatives, perhaps Gretchen could pull herself out of her own rut. Now, envision what happens with a change in the social setting and development of a goal.

> *Lisa, Gretchen's neighbor, comes out of her house shouting, "Want to jumprope with me, Gretchen?" Gretchen's eyes brighten, a wide smile appears, and she zooms across the lawn with unlimited energies.*

Here, through a change in the social setting, Gretchen has found a goal—a purpose for that moment. This has transformed her into a person with a zest for life. The difference is a goal that gives her focus and revitalizes her.

The encourager believes that a change in goals or even the development of new goals parallels a person's energy level. New goals carry with them rich possibilities. Sometimes, a person lacking a goal can fall prey to another who offers a goal, albeit a misdirected one.

> *Clark, the son of a wealthy businessman, had all his material needs well taken care of, but his personal and social needs were ignored. His hard-driving, successful parents allowed him to buy whatever he wanted—the only thing they didn't have for him was time.*
>
> *Clark went to college and, because he lacked direction and purpose, fell in with a group whose members experimented with drugs. The group members seemed to care for him (at least they allowed him to be a part of their activities) and he was "noticed." The experience felt good. He now takes drugs to maintain the approval of the group. Clark is at this point driven by the goal of being constantly high.*

The use of drugs has become an obsession, a goal for Clark. In this case the goal is misdirected and his energies are mobilized in a negative direction.

The encourager believes that it is vital to help the turned-off person develop positive, responsible goals. When this happens, all the person's energies can become utilized in the process of achieving these goals.

ASSUMPTION V: THE INDIVIDUAL ACTS ACCORDING TO THE WAY HE OR SHE VIEWS THE WORLD

What the encouraging person is concerned about is not how the world is, but how the discouraged person views it. This is his "inner reality"; it is what determines behavior. In Dinkmeyer and Dreikurs we read:

> Man can only be understood in terms of his phenomenological field. We are influenced not by the facts, but by our particular interpretation of them. It is more important to know how the child feels than to know the concrete details of his act. All behavior makes sense to the individual in terms of the way in which he views the world.
>
> To work effectively in guidance, teaching, counseling or therapy, one must be cognizant of the child's subjective view, his "private logic." Our senses receive images that are interpreted subjectively. Each individual interprets reality in a slightly different manner Thus, private logic can be contrasted with common sense. These personalized meanings help us to see the importance of viewing behavior subjectively instead of objectively.

The significance of past experience depends on the way in which the individual has come to interpret it; this knowledge is vital for understanding and influencing behavior. It is more vital to know how a person uses his ability than to know what his ability is. . . .[3]

A key statement to consider is, "All behavior makes sense to the individual in terms of the way in which he views the world." In seeking to understand a person's goals, you'll probably find that what may appear at first to be illogical is quite logical to this individual. Thus it is futile to use blame, criticism, or lecturing to try to change his behavior. Sometimes, people may cite goals, yet work against achieving them. So the encouraging person must allow for the possibility of unconscious motivation, as well. This is the unrealized part of the goal.

Jeffrey, 19, is put on probation for robbery and is told that if he violates the probationary rules he will surely go to prison. Two days later, Jeffrey is caught red-handed in a burglary. He doesn't even attempt to escape. Everyone is confused by his actions.

If you asked Jeffrey if he wanted to get caught, he'd certainly say "No." Consciously, he didn't want to get caught, but unconsciously, his goals were quite different. His behavior made sense in terms of the goals, conscious and unconscious, of the total person. It is only through knowledge of these goals that the encourager can help another person.

In Chapter 3 we discussed helping people learn to consider optional ways of viewing their world by the enrichment of their perceptual alternatives. The "turned-on" person has the ability to perceive all the possibilities in his/her situation and then act in the most positive and responsible way.

[3]Ibid., p. 11.

YOUR OWN NEEDS: INTERFERENCE OR AID TO THE ENCOURAGEMENT PROCESS?

The encouraging person makes a commitment. That commitment is to help the self-defeating person view life differently, establish goals, make an effort to reach these goals, take personal responsibility for his/her effort, evaluate this effort, and develop self-rewarding and self-encouraging skills. (We will discuss these distinct steps in the turning-on process in the next chapter.) Your role as an encourager is to create the atmosphere that is most likely to result in these goals. However, it is vital that you keep reminding yourself that *THE RESPONSIBILITIES FOR ACCOMPLISHING THESE GOALS ALWAYS LIE WITH THE DISCOURAGED PERSON!* If it happens that the encouragement process is unsuccessful, it is only an indication that there might be a more appropriate approach; it is not a reflection of your personal worth. Your purpose is not to prove how intelligent you are; nor should you take credit for another person's growth. Your goal is to try to provide the best possible social circumstances within which that person can reach his/her goals.

SUMMARY

In this chapter we have discussed five assumptions you as an encourager must accept before you can help others achieve a "turned-on" lifestyle. These assumptions provide the most important guidelines in your refinement of the art of turning people on through encouragement. The essential point of all of the assumptions is that it is the *individual* you must consider; and that this individual exists as a social being; functions as a complete person with goals, purposes, and values that motivate him/her; and acts according to the way he/she views the world.

Again it has been stressed that the encourager's purpose is to *enable the turned-off person to work toward his/her own goals*, not to enhance a personal feeling of importance, superiority, or success or even to feel less worthwhile if the effort should fail.

Questions

1. Why can't an encouraging person focus on the needs of an entire group in the "turning-on" process?

2. What is the "raw material" for the encouragement process?

3. What is a possible problem associated with Assumption I?

4. Can you give an example from your own experience in which the social payoff has affected your motivation?

5. What is often the reason for feelings of boredom and lassitude?

6. What relationship does a person's view of the world have to the scope of his perceptual alternatives?

Chapter 5

The Art of Encouragement: A Systematic Approach

This is the chapter in which we "put it all together." We have examined the process of discouragement—how it develops in people—and we have looked at its symptoms. Then we discussed the importance of helping self-defeating individuals learn how to develop perceptual alternatives, become more open to newer, more positive ways of thinking and behaving. In the last chapter we set down five assumptions that should be basic in our thinking as we become encouraging people. Now it is time for us to get down to the major business of determining a systematic approach to turning people on through encouragement.

There are six main phases in the turning-on process. As you will observe, they are quite overlapping and flexible. To attempt to treat them as "rules" is to miss the concept expressed in Chapter 3 about perceptual alternatives. The encouraging person is more interested in the *pace and direction as it is established by the discouraged person* than in following a fixed, inflexible program.

We will discuss each of the following phases in this core chapter of the book:

Creating the ideal encouraging relationship
Deciding what to focus on in the discouraged person
Facilitating decision-making
Encouraging action
Encouraging self-evaluation
Encouraging self-encouragement

CREATING THE IDEAL ENCOURAGING RELATIONSHIP

Unconditional Positive Regard

The encouragement relationship must be built on an attitude of complete acceptance—what Carl Rogers refers to as "unconditional positive regard."[1] This reflects an attitude of "I accept you exactly as you are, with no conditions whatsoever." Most of our everyday relationships have an element of qualification in them. The inference is that as long as you do thus and so for me, I will accept you—but if you do not meet my conditions, I can no longer accept you.

> *Sally comes home with two D's on her report card. Her father fumes and calls her a lazy, stupid child. Her mother says, "Oh, how could you do this to me? Don't you care? Go straight to your room!"*

This is clearly a conditional relationship. Sally's acceptance is based on school grades—her parents haven't made a single effort to find out how Sally feels, or *why* she got two D's.

In an unconditional relationship, one is accepted "with-

[1] *On Becoming a Person* (Boston: Houghton Mifflin Company, 1961).

out any strings attached." The encouraging person allows people to be themselves and applies no pressure on them to change. In fact, this person can even be accepting of a *refusal* to change. As an encourager you will need to resist pushing for changes in the turned-off person; this attitude would indicate that your needs have become more important, and would present a strain in the relationship. Remember, it was just such conditional relationships that helped to create the discouragement in the individual in the first place. In an interesting book about her relationship with a disturbed youngster, Virginia Axline provides an excellent example of unconditional positive regard. (In this particular incident the author's caution was interpreted as a demand by the youngster and created a temporary setback in the relationship.)

He noticed a can of scouring powder on the shelf above the sink. He climbed up and got it.

"What is in this can?" he asked.

"Scouring powder," I said.

He smelled it, shook some out in his hand, looked at it, then suddenly put it in his mouth to taste.

"Oh no, Dibs!" I exclaimed. "That's scouring powder. Not good to taste!"

He turned and looked at me coldly. This sudden reaction of mine was inconsistent.

"How can I tell how it tastes unless I taste?" he asked with dignity.

"I don't know of any other way," I told him. "But I don't think you ought to swallow it. It isn't good to taste."

He spit it in the sink.

"Why don't you rinse your mouth out with some water?" I suggested. He did. But my reaction disturbed him. He put the scouring powder back on the shelf and gave me a cold look.

"I'm sorry, Dibs," I said. "I guess I just didn't think. But I didn't like to see you take such a big mouthful of scouring powder."

He bit his lip, walked over to the window. His sensitive armor was ready to be put on quickly when his feelings were hurt.[2]

The encouraging relationship is a unique experience for both individuals involved because of its implication of no demands—of allowing people to be the way they are. It is only when you give people the freedom to choose *not* to grow that they can freely choose growth.

Nonblaming Attitude

Discouraged people have been hurt. They have *learned* to develop negative attitudes and behaviors. An encourager believes that they would act differently if they could see advantages or benefits that might result from their behavior. This makes it essential that criticism, blame, and punishment are not a part of the relationship. Self-defeating people have been blamed by almost everyone with whom they've been in contact and *this didn't work*. Without these negatives, they need not put up a front, be defensive, lie, or pretend to be people who they are not out of fear. They can be themselves, maybe for the first time in their lives. When the encouraging person can establish this sort of a positive environment, the "turned-off" person has something secure and good to return to after facing the battles of the world and after taking sometimes threatening risks. Remember, the encouraging person believes that discouraged people would act differently if they felt confident that they could.

[2]*Dibs: In Search of Self* (Boston: Houghton Mifflin Company, 1964). Used by permission of the publisher.

Empathy

The most important ingredient in an encouraging relationship, as we mentioned in an earlier chapter, is an open-mindedness, a willingness to try as hard as you can to feel everything the discouraged person is feeling. Thus it is necessary that you listen carefully and review with the person what you think you've heard. You must "target" how (s)he feels. Your perceptions may be close or quite distant; if they differ, you must try to develop an alternate way of perceiving the other viewpoint. Try to get right on target in identifying that person's feelings.

DISCOURAGED PERSON: *I don't want to go to school anymore!*

ENCOURAGING PERSON: *You don't like school? (missed target)*

DISCOURAGED PERSON: *Oh, I like it, but I'm just afraid I'm going to fail.*

ENCOURAGING PERSON: *It would really be frightening for you to fail and so you're considering not going back at all. (bull's-eye)*

DISCOURAGED PERSON: *Right!*

The encouraging person took a risk in trying to understand the discouraged person and at first was wrong. With more information, an ability to back away from the first conclusion (since it wasn't validated), and the use of alternative perceptions (requiring an open mind), the "target" was hit the second time. The encouraging person was now, temporarily, able to walk in the other person's shoes—all of a sudden his behavior, thoughts, and feelings made sense. But a word of caution: It is important never to lose sight of your *own* world, since you cannot be effective in helping the discouraged individual develop perceptual alternatives if you view everything the way that person does.

Confidence

Encouraging people have confidence in those they help. They believe that if they provide the conditions that will maximize growth, chances are excellent that self-defeating individuals will begin their search for themselves and their new identities. Therefore it is essential to help such people to realize that their reasons for past failure may have been factors outside themselves, or to lack of enough interest on their part. Frequently, discouraged people believe that they simply lack the ability to change. Continually, students who have been "failures" in high school achieve great success in college because it wasn't a lack of ability, but a lack of interest that had made them poor students. This idea may have been reinforced by teachers. Often it is a simple matter of the encouragement of one individual who *believes* in the discouraged person that makes the difference in attitude. Confidence is the key word. Confidence from someone else breeds confidence in self.

This area of encouragement is not without its problems. Turned-off people sometimes distrust someone who tries to help. Why shouldn't they? Perhaps no one else in their lives has believed in them. Suspicious and hurt people may even wonder, "What's in it for him/her?" Sometimes the discouraged person even feels guilty. "How can I ever live up to his/her belief in me?" or "This person really doesn't know me—if (s)he did, (s)he couldn't possibly believe in me." Such self-effacing or critical comments are only symptoms of the deep nature of the wound. The "I don't want your help" mask may be hiding a feeling of "I'm not worthy of your help" or "You may not be sincere and I'll only suffer greater hurt when you leave me." For example,

> *Mr. A was a counselor working with elementary school children in a "social restoration" class. One day he was confronted by a 10-year-old classified as a "school phobic" who*

said, *"The only reason you're nice to us is because you're getting paid for it."*

This reaction reflected a total feeling of worthlessness. Time, continued encouragement, and belief in the individual are all needed in convincing an unhappy person of your sincere confidence. The importance of getting the discouraged individual to believe in your confidence in him is expressed perfectly in the words of a college student who recently told an encouraging person:

> I took a chance and went out for the job interview. I knew that you felt I could present myself positively, but I wasn't quite sure myself. Boy, did the man like me! I got the job and start in three weeks. I just had to rush in and tell you because I knew you'd be anxious to hear about it.

Discouraged people must come to believe that you are genuinely interested in their progress—that you really care. Think of it this way: when you accomplish something, such as an "A" in school or a raise in salary, you don't feel complete until you can tell someone about it—you want to share. That, and the feeling you have at that moment, is what it's all about. Discouraged people lack someone to talk to about their successes. When people come to you with a brightness in their eyes and an eagerness to present something to you, think about how they might be feeling, and respond accordingly. Your response brings us to another condition of encouragement—enthusiasm.

Enthusiasm

Besides being nondemanding, empathetic, and having confidence in people, the encouraging person should be able to express sincere enthusiasm. If you understand—really understand—what people are telling you when they proudly present their report card or their prize or their new idea—if you have real empathy—you can't possibly be anything but enthusiastic. Encouraging people are not afraid of their positive emotions and can express them to other people.

You as an encourager should be aware of how vital are your reactions to the discouraged person's ideas. After all, he "took a risk" and told you. This is healthy and a real compliment to you. An enthusiastic, nonevaluative response to his feelings will give this person the courage to take a risk again. (We will be discussing nonevaluative listening shortly.) Your reaction to what he says may determine whether or not he pursues goals (growth) or gives them up (stagnation). A comment uttered in a monotone or a neutral or disinterested facial expression can really turn off someone who is already in doubt about his or her abilities and worth.

Everyone needs to compare their ideas with those of others—this is a way of authenticating one's own reactions. If a person stops communicating with others because they consistently turn him/her off, this can have seriously damaging effects. In what is called Social Comparison Theory, this need to express oneself to others is acknowledged to be a vital one:

> People need to evaluate their opinions and abilities and when no objective means are available, they do so by comparing their reactions with those of other people. The more uncertain people are, the more is their need for social comparison.[3]

When this need to "refer" to the ideas and opinions of others is received well—i.e., with sincere interest and enthusiasm —the result is an *encouraged* person, one who will be more inclined to take a risk in sharing in the future.

[3]Leon Festinger, "A Theory of Social Comparison Processes," *Human Relations*, 2 (1954), 117–40.

Nonevaluative Listening

As Carl Rogers points out, human beings have a tendency in everyday conversation to immediately evaluate, rather than to try to understand what the other person is saying.[4] In the ideal relationship, the encourager takes what the discouraged person has said and considers the thoughts and feelings behind the statement. The rightness or wrongness of the comment is not what is important—what is important is understanding what the discouraged person is saying.

DISCOURAGED YOUNGSTER: *You never let me do anything and always let Tommy do whatever he wants to.*

PARENT: *What do you mean? You are absolutely crazy! Last week we took you to the movies; the week before to the playground.*

DISCOURAGED YOUNGSTER: *Yes, but I really wanted to go to the baseball game and you're taking him instead.*

You can imagine how long this debate can go on—it could blossom into a real battle. In this case, the parent isn't interested in understanding, but only in "proving" and "evaluating." No amount of proof can change this discouraged child's reaction. Now consider the following, nonevaluative approach:

DISCOURAGED YOUNGSTER: *You never let me do anything and always let Joey do whatever he wants to.*

PARENT: *Sometimes you feel that I'm unfair to you. It seems to you that I let your brother do things that you'd like to do. This makes you angry.*

DISCOURAGED YOUNGSTER: *It sure does!*

In this conversation the parent and child are in agreement. They *both* recognize and accept the child's anger as a reality.

[4]On Becoming a Person.

The child is understood and there is no need to continue such a debate.

Here is another evaluative dialogue:

DISCOURAGED YOUNGSTER: *Charlie beat me up in front of all the other kids.*

PARENT: *What did you do to* him?

DISCOURAGED YOUNGSTER: *I didn't do anything. Why are you always getting on me?*

PARENT: *Don't tell me you didn't do anything. Nobody just goes and beats up on someone else without a reason.*

Now contrast that *evaluative* approach to this *listening* approach:

DISCOURAGED YOUNGSTER: *Charlie beat me up in front of all the other kids.*

PARENT: *That must have made you feel embarrassed.*

DISCOURAGED YOUNGSTER: *Sure did! Boy, I got real mad. He beat me up just because I called him a name.*

PARENT: *You feel as though he was unfair in doing something like beating you up just for name-calling.*

DISCOURAGED YOUNGSTER: *Yeah.*

So, in *nonevaluative listening*, you pay attention to what the discouraged person says and try to understand. Don't let judgments enter into the picture, if at all possible. Listen carefully to the words and try to *translate the words into feelings*.

Now try some nonevaluative response exercises. Remember, translate the words into feelings that the discouraged person is trying to convey.

EXERCISE 1.

DISCOURAGED YOUNGSTER: *Oh, you promised yesterday, Mom, that we would go to get ice cream when Dad got home from work today. Now you tell me that he has to work late!*

NONEVALUATIVE RESPONSE: *(fill in):* _____

_____

EXERCISE 2.

DISCOURAGED PERSON *(on her birthday)*: *I couldn't wait to see you today because of how important this day is to me, and you forgot all about it!*

NONEVALUATIVE RESPONSE: _____

_____

EXERCISE 3.

DISCOURAGED YOUNGSTER: *I hate you, Dad. You never want to play baseball with me anymore.*

NONEVALUATIVE RESPONSE: _____

_____

Evaluation of the Quality of the Ideal Encouraging Relationship

In evaluating the quality of an encouraging relationship we can postulate three general "levels." You can easily apply the ideas expressed in the following list to a relationship in which you are trying to encourage a specific person.

Level I evaluations indicate that work needs to be done to improve the relationship. Suggestions and readings are listed to help bring the concept into focus. If, after re-reading and an examination of your own needs there is no improvement, alternative approaches may be more appropriate. If there is improvement to Level I, move on.

Level II evaluations signify the minimum conditions suggested for an encouraging relationship. They are adequate, but a little additional work is listed. From that point, move on.

Level III evaluations indicate an "ideal and productive factor" in the quality of the encouraging relationship. From that point, move on.

1. *EVALUATION OF UNCONDITIONAL POSITIVE REGARD*

———*Level I:* I find this person to be obnoxious and clearly asking for the miserable life (s)he's created. I really feel that little can be achieved by spending time with this person. At times I'm convinced (s)he's lying and this angers me. (S)he does things constantly that I don't like.

———*Level II:* I get upset with this person, but when I think about it, I realize that (s)he can act the way (s)he chooses. Sometimes I feel that I've reached my limits with this person, but somehow or other I can pull myself together again.

———*Level III:* If there are times that this person is doing things I don't like, that's my problem, not his/hers. I can let this person run his/her own life and be him/herself. Although I would like things to be different, I can accept things the way they are. If I were this person, with all his/her circumstances, I might act the same way.

If you rate at Level I, then:

a.   Reread Chapter 5 (Unconditional Positive Regard), pp. 88–90.)

b.   Think about your own *needs* to make this person change. From where are the *pressures* coming? Can you alter your needs, or develop alternative ways of perceiving the pressures?

c.   Consider the possibility of an alternate approach other than encouragement.

d.   If you sense that the relationship has worsened, perhaps it would be proper to discuss the situation with someone else.

If you rate at Level II, then:

a.   Reread "Unconditional Positive Regard" (pp. 88–90).

b.   Move on to evaluating #2—the Nonblaming Attitude.

If you rate at Level III, then:

a.   Move on to evaluating the Nonblaming Attitude.

2. *EVALUATION OF THE NONBLAMING ATTITUDE*

————*Level I:* At times, I blame, criticize, lecture, or use sarcasm with this person.

————*Level II:* Although I feel the need to blame, criticize, or lecture, I don't express these ideas.

————*Level III:* I do not feel or express blame, criticism, or sarcasm in the relationship.

If you rated yourself at Level I, then:

a.   Reread "Discouragement through Intimidation" (pp. 53–56).

b.   Reread "Nonblaming Attitude" (p. 90).

c.   Consider your own *needs* in this relationship

(e.g., to dominate, to control, to be successful, to protect).

d.   Look for an alternate approach to helping.
e.   Seek out someone else to help this person.

If you rated yourself at Level II, then:

a.   Reread "Nonblaming Attitude" (p 90).
b.   Go on to evaluation of Empathy.

If you rated yourself at Level III, then:

a.   Go on to evaluation of Empathy.

3.   *EVALUATION OF EMPATHY*

————*Level I:* I have no idea where this person is at. I rarely hit the "Target" and it is extremely difficult for me to put myself in this person's place.

————*Level II:* At times I feel I know where this person is coming from and occasionally I hit the "target," but it is still hard for me to identify or put myself in his/her place.

————*Level III:* Most of the time I am able to understand and "target" this person. His/her behavior really appears to make sense to me as I consider the way (s)he views life.

If you rate at Level I, then:

a.   Reread "Empathy" (p. 91).
b.   Reread "Discouragement through Insensitivity" (pp. 47–51).
c.   Consider, "How different are my background, life experiences, and values from this person's?" If they are too different, it might be extremely difficult for me to identify. Perhaps someone else closer to this person's experiences might be a more appropriate encourager.

If you rate at Level II, then:
  a. Reread "Empathy" (p. 91).
  b. Go on to evaluating #4—Confidence.
If you rate at Level III, then:
  a. Go on to evaluating #4—Confidence.

4. *EVALUATION OF YOUR CONFIDENCE IN THE PERSON'S ABILITY TO CHANGE*

————*Level I:* I seriously doubt that this person has the ability and motivation to make changes. It appears to me that the discouraged signs are too deeply embedded. So far, I've found the relationship to be totally unproductive and it looks as though it will continue that way.

————*Level II:* This person appears to talk about change, but doesn't always follow through. Consequently, I'm just not sure whether there will be any significant changes. However, I don't doubt that this person has the ability and motivation.

————*Level III:* This person is and will continue making progress. It's obvious that (s)he tells me about his/her successes and failures. I feel that this person knows I believe in him/her.

If you rate at Level I, then:
  a. Reread "Confidence" (pp. 92–93).
  b. Reread "Unconditional Positive Regard" (pp. 88–90) and "Nonblaming Attitude" (p. 90).
  c. Consider using an alternate approach.

If you rate at Level II, then:
  a. Reread "Confidence" (pp. 92–93).
  b. Reread "Unconditional Positive Regard" (pp. 88–90).
  c. Go on to evaluating #5—Enthusiasm.

If you rate at Level III, then:

    a.   Go on to evaluating #5—Enthusiasm.

5. *EVALUATION OF ENTHUSIASM*

————*Level I:* It's almost impossible for me to get excited about this person's concerns. I can't get myself to express anything positive to this person.

————*Level II:* Although I recognize how important some of the things are that this person talks about to him/her, I can't quite get the total feeling. Most of the times I am able to show positive emotions to this person's feelings about his/her ideas.

————*Level III:* I'm able to identify with this person's feelings behind his/her ideas. I constantly try to express my awareness of these feelings.

If you rate at Level I, then:

    a.   Reread "Enthusiasm" (pp. 93–94).

    b.   Reread "Discouragement through Silence" (pp. 51–53).

    c.   Consider your own needs which may inhibit you from understanding and expressing positive feelings to this person.

If you rate at Level II then:

    a.   Reread "Enthusiasm" (pp. 93–94).

    b.   Reread "Discouragement through Silence" (pp. 51–53).

If you rate at Level III:

You have concluded evaluating the quality of the encouragement relationship.

Be sensitive to these five areas at all times in the relationship. A Level I functioning in more than one of these areas may impair the relationship.

It is now time to take a look at what to *focus on* in the discouraged person, the second phase in the "turning-on" process.

DECIDING WHAT TO FOCUS ON IN THE DISCOURAGED PERSON

Having established the ideal encouraging relationship, your next logical step is to try to understand the self-defeating person better. To do this, you will have to focus on certain aspects of that person so you can decide what his/her discouraged behaviors are and how you can best help him/her to effect a change. After we have examined some of the focal areas, we will briefly review your progress up to this point.

Thoughts, Actions, and Feelings (TAF)

There are three main routes that can be used to reach in the effort to understand a discouraged person. Some psychologists, such as Albert Ellis, suggest that it is important to understand the way a person views or thinks about life.[5] Others, like B. F. Skinner[6] and William Glasser,[7] take the position that the most appropriate means of understanding a person is to observe that person's behavior and actions. Finally, Rogers suggests becoming aware of the emotions or feelings of a person.[8]

It is not important to give more credence to any one of these approaches; none of them can claim a monopoly on success. What is important, however, is for you to become aware of these three areas—thoughts, actions, and feelings. The discouraged person has a disturbance that is exhibiting itself in at least one of these three areas, and this causes an overall problem leading to some of the symptoms we discussed in Chapter 1.

Here are some examples of expressed discouraged signs, with an indication of the problem area you might initially focus on.

[5]*Reason and Emotion in Psychotherapy* (Secaucus, N.J.: Lyle Stuart, 1962).
[6]*About Behaviorism* (New York: Knopf, 1973).
[7]*Reality Therapy* (New York: Harper & Row, 1975).
[8]*On Becoming a Person.*

JOHN *(age 24)*: *I have these, like, uh, butterflies in my stomach. It's the craziest thing and I can't explain it.*

OBSERVED PROBLEM: *Feeling-related (uneasiness, anxiety).*

WILLIAM *(age 6)*: *I showed Tim. I punched him right in the mouth!*

OBSERVED PROBLEM: *Action-related (fight).*

MARY ANN *(age 45)*: *I think the whole world is against me.*

OBSERVED PROBLEM: *Thinking-related (false belief).*

In each brief example you've noticed a problem. The encourager, believing that the individual functions as a whole, can make some inferences about a person just by being able to focus on the most apparent problem area. For instance, in the second example, can you translate that action-related problem to a feeling-related one? You might say that William punched Tim in the mouth (action-related) because he was angry (feeling-related). This anger was created by what William told himself about Tim (thought-related). See the connection?

It is important to remember that inferences are not judgments or your moral evaluations of a situation. They represent an attempt on your part to better understand the "total" person by information that you have regarding small samples of that person (a statement, or an action, for example). These inferences may or may not be accurate. Only time will tell. For the balance of this book, the process of trying to understand the total person by focusing on one component of that person will be referred to as the *TAF translation*. The TAF (thought-action-feeling) translation will help you in your interrelationship with the discouraged person. Remember, focusing on one component doesn't mean you are excluding consideration of the other two—it is merely a useful method of determining what are the problems of the turned-off person as a *whole*.

In the following examples, try to determine the expressed problem and make the TAF translation:

HAROLD *(24, prison inmate)*: *This prison system is rotten. Four of us pulled the bank job and I'm the only one who got time for it.*

Is the prisoner's expressed problem thought-, action-, or feeling-related? Fill in the expressed problem in the proper blank. By generalizing on the one aspect of an individual, imagine what the individual's response might be in the other two areas:

Thought: _____

Action: _____

Feeling: _____

PARENT TO TEENAGER: *Taking the car keys away from you was the only way I could show you that I mean business about your reckless driving.*

Is the parent's expressed problem thought-, action-, or feeling-related?

Thought: _____

Action: _____

Feeling: _____

SUPERVISOR TO A FRIEND: *I've really been hurt by the fact that*

I didn't get that promotion. It makes me feel that the company doesn't appreciate me.

Is the supervisor's expressed problem thought-, action-, or feeling-related?

Thought: _____

Action: _____

Feeling: _____

It is important to remember that now you are more sensitive to the discouraged person's total personality. If you reach a roadblock in talking to an individual about his or her *behaviors*, you can then go to his or her *feelings* when you make the TAF translation. If that's too threatening, you can move into the areas of the person's *thinking*. You'll find that each discouraged person is different and presents one or the other aspects of self in the foreground. Many will talk out of their thoughts by opening up their sentences with, "I think." Many choose to describe their actions by saying, "I did." Others are most comfortable talking about feelings or saying, "I feel."

People's ability to accept and adjust to different TAF translations of themselves may very well be a positive indicator of their possibilities for growth. This is similar to their ability to develop perceptual alternatives.

Inconsistencies in the way a person expresses his thoughts, actions, and feelings are signs that the individual is not accepting his or her total self. An example of an inconsistency would include the discouraged person punching someone (action-related) while expressing real love toward

that person (feeling-related). Whenever the three components do not appear to match, there is a problem. The person is not ready to accept responsibility for his or her behavior. Hence, a discussion with the discouraged person is
appropriate if: (1) all the elements of the ideal encouraging
relationship are present; and (2) if the confrontation can be
handled in a nonthreatening way. But remember that at that
point you as the observer are taking responsibility for the
confrontation. It is only your feelings or thoughts that there
may be a TAF inconsistency. You could be wrong. Compare
these two types of confrontations:

> "First you say that you love Joe, then you punch him.
> That can't be."

> "I'm confused. On the one hand, you express love feel-
> ings toward Joe, but on the other hand you punch him.
> Could you help me straighten out something that isn't
> clear in my mind?"

In the first example, the observer begins the confrontation in a threatening way and acts out of the assumption that
his or her TAF translation is accurate. This attempt to
"force" the individual to justify inconsistencies causes stress
in the relationship.

In the second example, the observer is taking the "responsibility" for the problem. The observer is expressing
confusion ("this is my problem") and asking to be helped.
This approach is less threatening, yet will enable the discouraged person the opportunity to think through the problem.

Past Identities

The encouraging person believes that people see themselves in a certain way, in a certain image. This picture they
have of themselves may have no resemblance to how others
see them. So before you draw conclusions about people, keep

in mind that they themselves are the best reference source. They are, in effect, experts on themselves.

You must be sensitive to the person's past identities. Often this means you'll have to read between the lines. For example:

> I was always in trouble in high school, but I could always make the others laugh.
> *Possible Identity*: Class clown.
> My parents felt that it would be better if my older sister went to college instead of me, so I went to work.
> *Possible Identity*: Martyr.
> I never could go along with those stupid, out-of-date rules that the school has.
> *Possible Identity*: Rebel.
> I lost three jobs—in each case because the bosses didn't understand me.
> *Possible Identity:* Self-pitier.

Now *you* try some:

> Nobody in our block would ever tell *me* what to do—they knew I'd put them in their place.
> *Possible Identity*: _____
> I got all A's in school!
> *Possible Identity*: _____
> My parents were never home. They were out either drinking or dancing and most nights I went to bed not even knowing if they would be home the next day.
> *Possible Identity*: _____
> Everybody used to beat me up at school, so I was afraid to go.
> *Possible Identity*: _____

Although there may be a number of possible answers for the last four examples, how about bully, good student, rejected person, and weakling?

Statements like those in the examples give clues to people's impressions of themselves. Everyone has a number of identities which change in given situations. It is the way people view themselves that influences their behavior. You will find that if you are an encouraging person, discouraged people change their identity when they are with you.

It is important to point out that identities are not truth, but discouraged people are apt to consider them to be so. The person with the self-perceived identity of *poor student* may act on that identity—and hence perform poorly. That identity was developed out of a few experiences and generalized—it became inflexible, as did the behaviors associated with it. This is a perfect example of someone acting on a false belief about himself—and having that belief perpetuate the behavior that matches it.

A boy who wins arguments by fighting may be called a bully. Then he may come to identify *himself* as "bully" and act that identity out. It is difficult to shed an identity, because there is security in it. At least we know who we are, and that makes us *somebody*.

As a child, Nancy was very obese. The other children taunted her, calling her "Two-Ton" and "Fatso." Nancy developed an attitude of withdrawal, eventually becoming so shy she could hardly bear to speak in class. In her late teens her parents took her to a specialist, and Nancy succeeded in losing weight. At 22, she is a stunning, shapely young woman, but she is still painfully shy. Her identity as "Fatso" has remained with her.

The encouraging person must try to observe a person's past identities, positive as well as negative. Then he or she should talk about them with the discouraged person to see if the impression is accurate. (Our earlier discussions of empathy and targeting will be helpful in this area.) For example, in the following example, Frank learns about his identification of himself as a stupid person:

FRANK: *I failed in my junior year of high school and instead of going back, I quit.*

ENCOURAGING PERSON: *Sounds like you lost interest in school. Maybe you felt that school was too difficult and not worth the effort—am I right?*

FRANK: *Yeah, I had trouble all along in school.*

E.P.: *Did you have a favorite subject?*

FRANK: *Sure, I was real good in science. But that was only because we lived on a farm and a lot of things we talked about in school I knew about already.*

E.P.: *How did you do in science?*

FRANK: *Usually B's or C's.*

E.P. (*enthusiastically*): *Wow! Were you interested in science?*

FRANK: *Oh yeah, I could read about science all day.*

E.P.: *It sounds like you could do something when you were interested, when you wanted to do it.*

FRANK: *I don't know, I never thought of it that way.*

E.P.: *Sometimes, when people have bad experiences like failing, they blame themselves and feel that they are stupid. Yet it may be disinterest or boredom that's made them fail. The problem, of course, is that they never continue trying and never overcome this idea about themselves.*

FRANK: *You mean, maybe I'm not as stupid as I think?*

E.P.: *I mean that as long as you continue to see yourself* [past identity] *as stupid because of a few bad experiences, you'll never change. You seem to have built many ideas of yourself on possible "false building blocks." What's worse is that you've decided to move into that shaky house.*

FRANK: *Yes, but it's too hard to move out of. It's the only house that I have.*

Frank is in the process of changing his past self-defeating identity. With encouragement, he may change this to an identity as a person who fears risk-taking, thence to an identification of himself as a capable person who has it in his power to grow.

Claim to Fame

Everyone has attained many high points in life. These are times that have transcended other moments in their existence. Often, however, they are quite meaningless to the rest of the large, disinterested world. If a person grows up in a discouraging atmosphere, these high points are likely to be downplayed and forgotten. Remember what we said in the section on enthusiasm (pp. 93–94) about people's need to compare their feelings with those of others? The more discouraged a person is, the more (s)he tends to judge the importance of events and feelings by other people's reactions. If the response is apathy, the accomplishment is likely to be viewed as unimportant.

Jamie, 4, can swing higher on the swing than anyone in his neighborhood.

Eddie, 5, is the fastest preschool kid in his block.

Dan, a computer salesperson, never forgets a client's phone number.

Spike has the most unique car in town; a 1932 Ford roadster.

Bill, a beer salesperson, sells more of a certain brand of beer than anyone else in town.

Judy claims she cooks the best lasagna in town.

Alicia has the best-looking rose garden in the county.

Add some of your own and what you judge to be your friends' "claims to fame":

_____

_____

_____

_____

Get the point? These are meaningful and important facts to these people. However, if the rest of the world fails to recognize these things as important, the individual will eventually tend to disregard their value. The encouraging person must be sensitive to, and even encourage the person to talk about, his or her "claim to fame."

Children are frequently more able to talk about their sources of pride than are adults. Even a youngster who is troubled and "turned off" may respond eagerly to your desire to hear about the important things (s)he may have accomplished. However, with seriously wounded children and adults it may be quite different. They may resist or actually believe that they have nothing of which to be proud. It is only through a sincere, enthusiastic, interested listener willing to invest time in them that they may regain that fresh feeling of importance. As an encouraging person, you must be ready to actively seek out someone else's "claim to fame."

Present Strengths

By this point in the encouragement process, discouraged people are beginning to emerge as real human beings. You start to recognize them as people with past successes and failures, sources of pride, identities, unrealized hopes and goals. They have many wounds to be healed. They are to be seen, remember, as complete persons. Consequently, if one part of them is hurt, they are totally affected. By the same token, if one part of them is refreshed, they are totally refreshed.

If all the conditions making for an ideal encouraging relationship are present (acceptance, confidence, nonblaming attitude, enthusiasm, nonevaluative atmosphere, and empathy), you are now ready to focus on a person's present strengths. It is likely that by now this individual is quite different from what he/she was in the beginning of the relationship. At this point people feel much better about themselves and lose some of their inhibitions about talking honestly about themselves. Because of their willingness to open up and talk nonapologetically, you'll get a more well-rounded version of them at this stage. They are more inclined to "focus" more realistically on their strengths and weaknesses. In encouragement, you center on their "viewed" strengths. In building up people's strengths you can assist them to face and cope with any weaknesses. Once they begin to do this they can see the light at the end of the dark tunnel. You'll even notice that they may start to "model" your enthusiasm. Their energy level has increased, and some alternative purposes in life start developing. Often, when discouraged people experience this new surge of positive self-belief, an unrealistic idealism may occur. In a sense, they start to set what appear to be unattainable goals. This is similar to what a child does and is not based totally in reality. An encouraging person understands and recognizes that this is a natural part of the process. The formerly turned-off people are, in a sense, filling in gaps for the things in childhood that they may never have experienced. Don't take it away from them again!

Your conversations with emerging persons should still continue to focus on their positive aspects. But at this point, they may be ready to discuss their potentialities in the light of external reality.

One of the pitfalls helpers fall into is to "expect" others to be at a certain point. It is vital to view others in a realistic sense—that is, where they are now, *at this moment*. You want them to be somewhere else, but they aren't. Johnny may know how to add single-digit numbers without any problem. If your *immediate* goal is to get Johnny to be able to divide three-digit numbers, you are setting him up for sure failure. You must take his readiness into consideration and be aware that there are necessary intermediary steps along the way that will maximize his possibility of success. At this time you can help the person to consider long-range goals as well as short-range ones by encouraging him/her to find the logical steps, prepare a tentative plan for him/herself.

Formerly discouraged people generally are now more prepared to accept the world. Your confidence in them and your recognition of their positive traits provide for them the support for the "real-world" test.

Review of Progress

When you come to this point with a person, you mustn't take anything for granted. You should stop and think where the discouraged person was when the relationship began. It is important for you to discuss with the emerging person his or her progress. Consider the following possible discussion questions:

"Do you feel differently about yourself than you did
——— weeks ago?"
"How are you different?"
"What do you do now that you wouldn't have done before?"
"Where would you like to go from here?"

It is essential for you to tell the growing individual how he or she has progressed from your perspective. As we have stressed time and again throughout the book, *knowing* something positive about a person and *communicating* it to that person are two different things.

At this point, then, you have (1) accumulated a list of positive traits of the person; and (2) *communicated* that knowledge to the individual. Enhanced by someone else's confidence in them and focusing on the positive aspects of themselves, emerging people can now start to think in terms of pluses rather than minuses. They are ready to experience life more fully. Now it is time to consider the following questions for yourself:

> Can I allow this person to be the way he or she wants to be, rather than the way *I* want him/her to be?
> Do I know this person's strengths?
> How accurate are my TAF translations?
> Have I noticed any inconsistencies in the TAF translations?

If you've come to this point with discouraged people, congratulations, but hang in there a little longer. **You have now helped people to experience life with all of its potential risks. In a sense, you've taken away some of their security. They need an encouraging person more than ever right now. They need support and encouragement should they fall.**

FACILITATING DECISION-MAKING

The responsibility for changing their lives lies solely with discouraged people themselves. Any attempt to take responsibility or make decisions for them only carries them deeper into discouragement over the long run. Remember the discussion of the dominators in Chapter 2—and how they inevitably breed either further weakness or rebellion in the people around them. Every gesture on your part is appropriate only if it has the goal of helping people to encourage *themselves*.

Your first responsibility is to make your best effort in providing the proper atmosphere for personal growth to occur. These conditions are listed earlier in this chapter. Your next responsibility is to gather the great amount of valuable information you have into some meaningful understanding of the total person. Then you are in a better position to help the discouraged person search for alternatives.

At this point, it is appropriate to discuss the difference between internal and external reality (Chapter 3) with the person you are helping. Explore with him or her things that (s)he would have liked to do in life, but didn't. What were the person's reasons for not doing these things? Discuss whether the resistance to action was based on external or internal realities. Here, you'll get a feel for the person's present sense of mastery or control over his/her actions. At this moment in time in the relationship, people often feel much more in control of their lives than in the beginning phases. This gives them more of a feeling of freedom, which is exhilarating, but also a feeling of additional responsibility, which is frightening. Frequently, it is at this time that many people start to lose some of the discouraging signs we listed in Chapter 1. For example, people who formerly felt totally worthless may now feel that they have some positive traits and aren't all bad. This is a logical by-product of the encouragement process. After all, *they've been totally and unconditionally accepted; they have been honest and still retained your faith in them; you've been interested in their world; you've focused on a lot of positive traits about them;* and *you have confidence in them.* IS IT POSSIBLE THAT SOMEONE COULD COME OUT OF A RELATIONSHIP WITH THESE CONDITIONS PRESENT AND *NOT* BE THINKING AT LEAST A BIT MORE POSITIVELY ABOUT HIM- OR HERSELF?

As people's worlds of opportunities start to open up and

expand, it is helpful to encourage them to think about all the possible alternatives they have in their life. When they begin to recognize their many possibilities and options, they also become more open-minded and tolerant of others. Now even their manner of walk, dress, and grooming may change. Their energy level increases. They may start to talk about doing things that they would never have considered before. In general, they view life in a more positive way.

In the case of adults, it may be helpful to supplement what they have gained in this phase by letting them read Chapter 3 of this book. Since they are naturally developing perceptual alternatives, it is reinforcing for them to see their progress from this perspective.

Armed with the person's realization of an increased number of possibilities, you can encourage him/her now to consider a number of results or consequences of alternative actions. It is sometimes helpful to develop a chart and itemize actions with possible consequences. The person you are helping can be encouraged to do this same thing whenever (s)he reaches a *DECISION POINT*. For example:

Possible Action #1	*Possible Consequence of Action*
I can try for a job interview.	1. I may not get the interview.
	2. I may get the interview, but not the job.
	3. I may get the job, but not want it.
	4. I may get and take the job.

Possible Action #2	*Possible Consequence of Action*
I can stay home and not go for the interview.	1. I won't get the job.

Which alternative action (1 or 2) looks better?

Remembering that responsibility lies with people themselves for their own life, it is most desirable that you let them come up with their own course of action and their own possible consequences. However, at times, especially with people who lack a creative ability to foresee consequences or develop perceptual alternatives, it may be necessary to give some assistance *in the beginning*.

At the end of this phase, people may then enter into the "risk-taking" or "action" phase. You, as encourager, can't *make* this happen. All you can do is to try and create conditions to maximize the possibility of the occurrence of the next phase—in which you will encourage *action*.

ENCOURAGING ACTION

This is a difficult stage in the encouraging process. It's one thing to make a decision, another to act on it, as we all know. Discouraged people receive a lot of fringe benefits. After all, they live in a predictable world. Because they fear taking risks and making changes, in a sense they are comfortable. Each person looks at "newness" or "change" in a different way and with differing kinds of expectations. Remember the first day of school? Were you eagerly looking forward to a new experience or were you frightened about this situation with all its uncertainty? The various reactions may be due, in part, to whether you had an encouraging person with you or not.

At this stage, the formerly self-defeating individual may be well aware that in order to experience life fully, he must develop the ability to "shake himself up" and do things differently. But this competes with a past history of the fear of failure or concern over the uncertainty of new experiences. In a sense, the person's choices can be put on a balance sheet. Here is a hypothetical model of risk-taking:

Shall I Ask That Girl That I Like Out?

Yes, because. . .(Pluses)	*No, because. . .(Minuses)*
1. She may go out if I ask—she sure won't if I don't.	1. She may reject me.
2. I'll never know how she feels about me if I don't ask her out.	2. She may tell others that she rejected me.
3. I'd be proud to be with her.	3. If she goes out, maybe I'll wind up acting stupid.
4. We may have a good time.	4. Even if she goes out, we may not have a good time.

Discouraged people at this juncture in the encouragement process may be at a deadlock. Their choice—basically for growth or stagnation—depends upon the progress they have made so far. Are they ready to make the changes necessary for a full and responsible life? Are you prepared to follow through on the course you have set for yourself as an encourager?

There are three important areas involved with the phase in which action is encouraged: the attitude toward taking risks, the attitude toward successful efforts, and the attitude toward failures.

Risk-Taking

Erica, a fifth-grader, seldom completed her homework. The teacher knew that Erica had ability, and she finally became angry and said, "Erica, you know you can do this work —you're just being horribly lazy!" Erica's reaction was, "If I don't try—if I act lazy—at least the teacher won't know how stupid I am. I'd rather have her think I'm lazy than think I'm stupid."

There is always resistance to risk-taking in discouraged people, and the reason for this is usually fear of failure. Many people don't go out on dates, don't go to college, don't try math problems, don't learn how to drive, simply because they are afraid they might "mess up." But this is understandable when you consider that in the past they have been exposed to failure without any support. They felt people didn't believe in them, and consequently, they came to doubt their own ability to succeed at something new.

Successes

The encouraging person rewards any *effort* on the part of discouraged persons to change. *Any effort made represents a success.* The effort, however minute, is a sign of growth or "coming back to life." You as an encouraging person must be there at this valuable moment. You must make clear to discouraged people that *effort is the most important resource they have.*

Mrs. R, a third-grade teacher, was superb at rewarding effort. Whenever she asked a question she reminded the class that the only one wrong was the person who wouldn't try. Hands were universally raised in her class. Even if someone responded with an "incorrect" answer, he or she would be told, "I'm so glad you tried—there could be a better answer—think so that you can try again." The stigma associated with "being wrong" which leads eventually to discouragement or destroyed self-confidence wasn't present.

Dr. S, a psychologist, uses a technique with people who are unmotivated to seek work because of past failure in securing employment. He suggests that they set a goal, such as filling out three applications a day for three days straight. If they do that, they are successful. It isn't important at this point whether they are interviewed or find employment. After all, this is beyond their control. But what is important is that they have made an attempt; this is within their control. Dr. S achieves overwhelming success with this approach.

Each person has goals that he or she "focuses" on. The encouraging person, at this point, must pay attention to any effort discouraged persons make in an attempt to get out of their rut. This process involves, as well, a distinct change in vocabulary. Here are a few common statements and the encouraging person's equivalent vocabulary for each:

Everyday Statement	*Encouraging Statement*
1. How did you do?	1. I'm so glad you *tried!*
2. Did you get any work yet?	2. Have you *filled out* any applications yet?
3. Did you pass the test?	3. Did you *take* the test?
4. What did he say when you finally told him you liked him?	4. I'm happy you took the chance and told him you liked him!

Now you try some.

Everyday Statement	*Encouraging Statement* (fill in)
1. Mother to 4-year-old son: "Let me see the horse you drew."	1. _____ _____
2. Aunt to her 7-year-old niece: "Can you swim?"	2. _____ _____

Failures

Problems often result when people fail. After experiencing rejection, for example, people tend to exaggerate, or "catastrophize," in Albert Ellis' words. This is to view the situation irrationally. All that rejection means is that someone hasn't accepted the person—it *doesn't* mean that he or she is terrible and worthless.[9]

To accept the idea that a person is not a failure just

[9]For further exploration of this idea, see Albert Ellis and Robert A. Harper, *A New Guide to Rational Living* (Englewood Cliffs, N.J.: Prentice-Hall, 1975).

because (s)he has failed at something is to buck, in many cases, lifelong trends. As children, discouraged people may have been told that they were "good boys" or "good girls" when they brought home A's and "bad boys" or "bad girls" when they failed. Their worth has been judged according to their performance. Consequently, their conception of their own worth changes daily according to their successes and failures.

The encouraging person views an experience of failure not as a lowering of worth, but only as a suggestion that there may be an alternative way of approaching the problem. It is important for you as an encourager to believe and to communicate the feeling that just because someone fails it doesn't mean that that person is a failure.

At times of failure *and* of success, it is worthwhile to point out to the person you are helping his/her strengths, to focus on effort and change, rather than on failure and loss of worth. Here is a conversation in which the encourager helped a usually self-defeating individual to see that worth is not dependent upon success or failure. At the same time, the encourager was helping the other person learn to change his views on failure.

E.P.: *So, you had the highest grade in ninth-grade science?*

D.P.: *Yes, out of forty people.*

E.P.: *That must have made you proud!*

D.P.: *Sure did.*

E.P.: *Why? Did it make you better?*

D.P.: *No, but for a day I was the best in general science.*

E.P.: *Oh, yes, I can see that easily, but were you a better person?*

D.P.: *No, I guess not.*

E.P.: *You really weren't that much different as a person after the grade than you were before that grade, were you?*

D.P.: *No–I'm me either way.*

E.P.: *I agree–now what if you had received the lowest grade in the class? Would you have been less worthwhile?*

D.P.: *In science, yes!*

E.P.: *How about as a person?*

D.P.: *Oh no–not as a person.*

You as an encourager can help the other person learn that strengths and weaknesses are totally independent of worth. When discouraged people are in an atmosphere in which someone *believes in them, recognizes them, rewards their effort,* and *doesn't judge their worth,* they are more likely to take a risk—to take decisive action.

ENCOURAGING SELF-EVALUATION

Your goal as an encourager is to provide the ideal climate in which the discouraged person can grow. While doing this, you clearly recognize that the responsibility for growth always remains with the discouraged person. Any form of pressure on your part only shifts the responsibility from the discouraged person to you. The person must have free choice in his or her decision. Moreover, he or she must ultimately reach a point at which *self*-evaluation is possible.

One way to help someone learn to evaluate his/her progress and behavior is to encourage the formulation of concrete goals. These goals may be developed jointly by the individual and yourself. Visible measuring sticks help a person more clearly and objectively evaluate progress.

Eleven-year-old Sally had a problem completing her seatwork at school. The elementary counselor asked her, "How do you think you could become the best possible *Sally today in* school?" Sally responded, "By finishing my math, English, spelling, and geography." The counselor then asked, "How could you be the 'Needs Improvement' Sally?" She responded, "By doing nothing."

So, with the counselor's help, the following chart was drawn by Sally:

Best-Possible Sally	Medium Sally
4 Stars*	2 Stars
Finishes:	Finishes:
Math	Math
Geography	Geography
Spelling	
English	

Needs-Improvement Sally

No Stars
Finishes:
Nothing

With her teacher's permission, Sally was allowed to bring her work to the counselor each time she finished it. It is important in using such charts that the person be able to respond immediately. If Sally didn't finish her work, she couldn't visit the counselor or get the star. She also learned the lesson of goal-setting and self-evaluating. And remember, the goals were set by Sally herself.

This technique of developing a chart is very useful to many people. Before making such a chart, the person should be encouraged to think about all the things he could do within a specified period of time, say twenty-four hours. Next, he might write what he probably would do anyway

---

*Encouragers try to avoid candy, food, and money as rewards, stressing instead self-satisfaction for effort.

without the chart. Finally, he could write what he considered to be the most unproductive possibilities.

What I Possibly Could Do   *What I Do on a Typical*
(Ideal Self)   *Day (Probable Self)*

1. _____   1. _____

2. _____   2. _____

3. _____   3. _____

4. _____   4. _____

What Would Be the Least that I
Could Do (Unproductive Self)

1. _____

2. _____

3. _____

4. _____

After accomplishing something, the person is encouraged to "check it off." At the end of twenty-four hours, he now has a tool to evaluate his progress. This step is crucial. When someone becomes able to "self-evaluate," the time is near for the exit of the encourager. Again, the whole language of the conversations between the two is changing.

Comments such as these below now occur more frequently:

> Do *you* realize that *you* drew that chart, accomplished the goals, and checked them off by yourself? *You've* come a long way!
>
> What are some ways that *you* can develop to evaluate *yourself*?
>
> *You* must be so pleased with *yourself* when *you* think about how *you* have been able to change.

ENCOURAGING SELF-ENCOURAGEMENT

Whenever young children accomplish something, however small, they are excited, and want to show everyone. The first time they write a letter of the alphabet, for example, they exultantly exhibit their "creation." They are proud, and part of the enjoyment of a "successful" performance is in the sharing of that success.

At some point, however, in an optimal situation, youngsters start to "trust themselves" more—they are able to go for longer periods of time without any outside encouragement. They have, in effect, developed the ability to encourage themselves. (This is ideal, since often other encouragers are simply not around.) This should be the case when you are helping someone through the encouragement process. But if, after much encouragement, people are still not beginning to "stand on their own two feet," and seek more and more reassurance, this becomes an unhealthy situation. If you are creating more dependence than independence, the individual's growth will in the long run be thwarted.

If, however, you can keep the ultimate goal of self-encouragement in mind throughout the relationship, you can gradually help the discouraged person to take more and more responsibility. In effect, your goal as an encouraging person is *to not be needed*. This can be seen in the transition from statements like, "I'm really happy that you tried thus and so" to "Aren't *you* happy you tried thus and so finally?", or "How do *you* feel about trying thus and so?" This step is vital and the whole process of successful encouragement rests on clear-cut independence.

Signs of a Self-Encouraged Person

You may notice the following trends in the person who is developing the skill of self-encouragement:

1. The self-encouraged person willingly makes choices and takes responsibility for his/her choices.
2. The self-encouraged person is willing to trust his/her own evaluations of the world.
3. The self-encouraged person is becoming independent of you.
4. The self-encouraged person can willingly disagree with you.
5. The self-encouraged person shows less attention-seeking, revenge, and power-seeking behaviors.
6. The self-encouraged person tries new experiences, takes risks.
7. The self-encouraged person is more open and honest in discussing his/her thoughts, feelings, and actions.
8. The self-encouraged person is becoming totally open to new ideas.
9. The self-encouraged person recognizes the changing nature of the world and does not see the world only in black and white.
10. The self-encouraged person has an ability to accept, and doesn't ponder over, the inevitabilities of life —e.g., death, serious illness.

11. The self-encouraged person is more willing to be him/herself and has less of a need to wear a mask.

SELF-ENCOURAGEMENT IS THE ULTIMATE!

SUMMARY

In this core chapter of the book we have examined the six major phases of the encouragement process. These phases should not be seen as inflexible in their order and direction, but their ultimate goal is to enable the turned-off person to become fully responsible for him/herself, so that *you* will no longer be needed. Everything, including language and attitude, changes as the person proceeds through these stages and begins to become an encouraged human being.

The first thing an encourager must do is to establish the ideal encouraging relationship. To accomplish this, several conditions must be met. (1) You must have an attitude of complete acceptance—what is called *unconditional positive regard*—of the self-defeating person. (2) There must also be a *nonblaming attitude* so that the discouraged individual will no longer feel a need to lie, pretend, or wear a mask. (3) You as the encourager must use that most valuable of assets, *empathy*—be able to "target" the way the other person really feels. (4) Communicated *confidence* in the other person is absolutely vital—this enables that individual to strengthen his/her own feelings of self-worth. (5) Sincere *enthusiasm* is needed, for it authenticates the turned-off person's purpose and sense of value. (6) Finally, nonevaluative listening is important so that the turned-off person's real feelings can be expressed freely and without fear of censure.

The next step in the encouraging process is for you, as the helper, to decide what you are going to focus on in the discouraged person. The three main ways to understand this person are through observation of his *thoughts, actions, and feelings*. Through the TAF translation we are able to view the total person. The encourager must also find out the person's *past identities*, both positive and negative, in order to help him/her become able to build up the sense of self-worth. Everyone also has a *claim to fame* that should be investigated. Knowledge of meaningful events in a person's life helps us encourage a growing sense of meaning, value, and responsibility. Finally, the person's *present strengths* should be recognized and acknowledged (by that person, as well as by you, the encourager); the now-emerging positive person will be able to build on these to achieve a better and better outlook on life as a happy and responsible person.

The next phase is for the encourager to make it ever easier for the formerly turned-off person to make his/her own decisions. This responsibility lies solely *with that individual*; and as his/her self-mastery increases this ability will also grow.

Logically, encouraging the person, who is now becoming less and less negative and discouraged, to undertake his/her own actions, is next in the encouraging process. Here the person will become capable of taking more risks; (s)he will recognize realistic successes, and cease regarding *failing* as a sign of *failure*. At this stage you are beginning to be increasingly aware that your role as a helping person is nearing its end.

Encouraging self-evaluation follows—this capability is again the outcome of the person's growing self-confidence and assumption of greater responsibilities. Helping the individual establish goals is important at this phase. By now the person is no longer a discouraged, turned-off individual, but someone whose knowledge of and faith in him/herself is apparent.

Finally, when the person becomes able to encourage him/her*self*, to trust in his/her own decisions, judgments, ideas, and *self*, your time has come to exit. You are now at the culmination of *your* goal in the encouragement process—i.e., to not be needed.

Questions

1. What are the six main phases in the turning-on process?

2. Describe a situation in which *unconditional positive regard* exists.

3. Name the most important ingredient in an encouraging relationship. What is your ultimate aim as an encourager?

4. What is "targeting"? Write an imaginary mini-case in which someone misses the target in a conversation with a discouraged person; in which (s)he is right on target.

5. What is TAF, and how is it relevant to your interactions with the discouraged person? What is a TAF translation?

6. When a person is inconsistent in the expression of his thoughts, feelings, and/or actions, what does this suggest?

7. At what point in the encouragement process is it appropriate to discuss external and internal realities with the person you are helping? When would it be valuable for the person to read Chapter 3 in this book?

8. What single element promotes resistance to risk-taking in a discouraged person?

9. Describe some changes that take place in your manner of speaking as the other person begins to make an effort to get out of his/her discouraged rut? Give some examples.

Chapter 6

Encouragement: A Wrap-Up

I recently saw a kindergarten youngster wearing a button that read: "Catch Me Being Good." I wondered how many times people are noticed when they are just following the rules or doing what it is "assumed" they will do. It seems as though attention is reserved for the outstandingly good person or the bad person. The child who is sitting still in class isn't noticed; the one who is bouncing in his seat is. How significant it would be if one day we decided to focus only on desirable behaviors. Statements such as these would be heard at home:

> Wow! That was tremendous that you were here to eat right on time!
> When you opened the door for me earlier today, I thought it was super!
> Thanks for making dinner, Mom!
> Your face looks really clean. I'll bet you even washed behind your ears!

I was really pleased yesterday when you and your sister didn't have one fight from six o'clock to seven o'clock!

How neat—you put your clothing in the hamper without me telling you!

I noticed how you sat still during the whole dinner.

At school, you might hear these kinds of statements:

Class, Billy finished all of his work—so did Tommy and Sue. Let's clap for them.

Look at how quietly Johnny has been sitting for the last ten minutes.

Class, what were some of the good things that Sara did today?

The point is that we take most things for granted. We assume that Billy must finish all his work or that Jane must eat all her food—so we don't notice them when they do. We might carry on angrily if Billy *doesn't* do his chores, or if Jane knocks her spaghetti onto the floor, but this is negative attention. Positive behaviors don't get nearly as much notice.

To prove the validity of this assumption, try these exercises:

    1. Compliment someone about an aspect of his or her appearance a few times—e.g., "Your suit really looks sharp." Watch what happens! That person will become more conscious of his appearance when he knows he'll be around you.

    2. Compliment a child on some unique skill that he or she has—e.g., "You must be the world's foremost expert on the five multiplication table!" Well, you know what will happen. In your eyes she's important and she's proud and may even become better at the tables because she's been recognized for it.

In many cases vocational choices are made on the basis of being "noticed" for aspects or skills people have.

Children have great attention-getting weapons whenever they need to be recognized. They yell, fight, or throw things across the room. In many cases these are the same children who can never get attention with healthy behaviors. So they have resorted to antisocial ones. One elementary school counselor tried the technique of offering to call children's parents if they didn't exhibit these disruptive behaviors for one day. What an interesting response he received from the parents! The typical phone call went this way:

COUNSELOR: *This is the school guidance counselor. I'm calling about Tommy.*

PARENT: *What did that kid do now? Just wait until I get him home!*

COUNSELOR: *No, I'm calling to say he behaved well today.*

PARENT: *That brat is uncontrollable. Why, I'll. . . What did you say?*

COUNSELOR: *Yes, that's right—Tommy had a great day today and I promised that I would call to tell you. Make sure you tell Tommy I called.*

Yes, it's extra work—or is it, in the long run? This method doesn't take anything for granted. It assumes that people have free will and can do anything they want to do. They don't *have* to respond positively (our way), but if they do, we must notice it.

To wrap up the message of this book, here are some of the highlights of the major characteristics of the encouraging person:

- The encouraging person sees only individuals in the world. When faced with a "group" of people, (s)he views each individual as unique—with interests, problems, and goals that must be acknowledged.

- The encouraging person is a safe, totally accepting person. He or she believes that the discouraged indi-

vidual hasn't consistently experienced safe relationships—hence, a mask has developed. There is no
need for a mask around an encouraging person. The
self-defeating individual is accepted exactly as he or she
is.

● The encouraging person is skilled at looking for
uniqueness or differences in an individual. This is almost a second-nature skill that the helper develops
along the way. When his uniquenesses are noticed and
he begins to believe he is special and worthwhile, the
discouraged person can develop a sense of self-worth
and the courage to take risks and change.

● The encouraging person not only has faith in human
nature—more importantly, (s)he has faith in the discouraged individual. The communication of confidence
in the emerging person, and the time the helper spends
encouraging that person, has a healing effect. "This
person really believes in me, so I must be OK."

● The encouraging person is sincerely enthusiastic
about the growth of the discouraged individual—and
(s)he *communicates* this enthusiasm. This gives the other
person the feeling that someone cares and keeps
him/her on a steady course of progress.

● The encouraging person is ultrasensitive to the self-
defeated person's goals, values, and purposes, believing
that every behavior is significant and consequential. The
hurting person's past identities, both positive and negative, are acknowledged as clues to his/her present self-
evaluation. And the encourager helps this person learn
to see him/herself in a more favorable light.

● The encouraging person realizes that of great help in
building a new, more positive identity is knowledge of
the discouraged individual's past proud moments—his
or her "claim to fame." Encouraged to feel that (s) he
is worthwhile, the (formerly) self-defeating individual

now begins to change—to see perceptual alternatives that can be used in the formation of the new person. He or she begins to take risks, to formulate goals, to observe and evaluate this self-growth.

● The encouraging person is ready for this moment. In a sense, it's graduation day. But it can be frightening. What is needed is further encouragement and support, especially during those first few risks.

● The encouraging person is sensitive to an over-dependency in the relationship and now starts to help the person to develop self-encouragement. And one important by-product of this self-encouragement is that this new person begins to develop relationships with others in which he or she uses the same encouragement process that was used with him/her. This person has become an encourager!

ARE YOU THE RIGHT PERSON FOR ENCOURAGEMENT?

If you take on the project of encouraging someone who needs it, keep in mind that this is no small task. You are working against a number of years of trends in the opposite direction. You know you are the right person for the role if you can answer the following questions positively:

1. Can I be willing to accept this person's choice to stay the way he or she is?
2. Do I *really* believe in his or her *ability* to search for a purpose in life?
3. Do I have the *energy* to help?
4. Do I have the *time* to spend listening and understanding this person as totally as possible?
5. Can I *express* what I feel or am I too inhibited?

6. Am I willing to go off into what may appear to be meaningless directions in the beginning for the sake of *understanding*?
7. Can I allow this person to take risks *without judging* him or her?
8. Can I allow this person to reach the point at which he or she no longer needs me?

If you have answered yes to most of these questions, you are on your way. You are the right person for the job.

Oh, by the way—is it worth all the time and energy? I'll answer it this way:

1. Check the cost of keeping up a drug habit for a year.
2. Check the cost of keeping someone in a mental hospital for a year.
3. Check the number of suicides there are in the world every year.
4. Check the cost of housing a prisoner for a year.

So here we are, at the end of the encouragement process, looking at a person who has emerged from a depressing, disheartening, negative cocoon to become the happy, self-confident, encouraged human being we see now—one who will, as a part of his or her acknowledgment of the joy and privilege of living a full, meaningful, responsible life, willingly continues what you started—turning people on through encouragement.

NOW GO AHEAD—TURN SOMEONE ON—BE AN ENCOURAGING PERSON!

Epilogue

Since we started the book with a prologue to give you an idea of just what we were going to talk about in the book, it seems appropriate to have an epilogue, so that you can discover what you have learned by following the progress of a real case of a discouraged person. Now meet Elaine.

ELAINE: THE FRUSTRATED HOUSEWIFE

Elaine was 38 years old, married, and living with her husband John in a modest house with their three children. John was a steelworker who spent much of his time at work. He was socially active, going out three or four times a week to bowl, play cards, and drink beer at the local tavern. Elaine stayed pretty much at home and had only one or two close friends.

Elaine grew up the third youngest in a family of nine children. The parents weren't too well-off, so they encouraged the children to work early. Because of the struggles at home, Elaine had difficulties at school, even though she did manage to graduate from high school. Consequently, she never learned to see herself as a good student. After high school she started work as a waitress, a job she disliked.

When she was 22, she met John; they were married two months later. She had her babies early in the marriage, and never made any attempt to go back to work.

I first met Elaine through a friend of hers, Jana. Jana was a sophomore at our college. She said that she could closely identify with Elaine's experiences—two years before she had felt that she was in a similar rut. But she made a change and decided to go to school. The change was quite meaningful and she hoped that Elaine, with some encouragement, could have the same success. Consequently, Jana asked that I talk to Elaine about attending college.

First Interview

Elaine came into the office with Jana several days later. She looked as though she had been through a war. Her clothes were uninteresting and unstylish. Pronounced lines on her face, disheveled hair, and dark circles under her eyes suggested a great deal of fatigue and stress. Her physical condition gave me the impression that she was a much older woman.

COMMENTS: Frequently, a discouraged person uses quite a bit of energy "dodging" the world. This leaves the person less energy to take care of him/herself physically. Consequently, physical appearance is apt to go downhill. When one sees positive changes in dress or appearance, it may be a sign that the person is making progress; he or she may have an increased amount of resources available, because there is less focus on avoidance of being a "member" of the real world.

During the first discussion, Elaine spoke in a monotone, offering little more than "yes" or "no" responses. Occasionally she made a cynical comment about life. When I spoke about school she was apathetic, except for an expressed interest in psychology so she could "figure herself out." But she added that of course there wasn't enough time—with the kids, the house, and numerous other responsibilities that she felt.

COMMENTS: Already some of her identities were surfacing. The cynical comments reflected her perception of herself as someone who has been unfairly treated in life, a person who is thus a failure at finding a meaning to her existence. Her comment concerning an interest in psychology possibly indicated some concerns about her sanity. It was too early in the meeting, however, to make any definite assumptions.

The comment about the number of responsibilities she faced was inconsistent with the picture that Jana had painted of her. The impression that I had been given by Jana was that Elaine had been heavily criticized by her husband for her failure to do anything around the house. The encouraging person does not confront these inconsistencies at the early stages. Elaine was already used to confrontation and blame from her parents, the children, and her husband and this apparently hadn't worked. Within the encouragement framework, inconsistencies—even lies—are not challenged. The encourager must at this point be aware of all the motives a person may have for deception. It may reflect a need, a feeling of unimportance, or even a fear of telling the truth. The encouraging person must try to create a safe atmosphere in which a person won't find a need to deceive. But creating this atmosphere takes time.

After Elaine expressed an interest in psychology, albeit

from a negative motive, I talked about it. I became somewhat *enthusiastic* about her having this interest and talked to her a little about psychology. I also expressed concern about all her responsibilities at home. I asked if she had any time to read in that difficult schedule and she suggested, "Not a big book." I recommended a few paperbacks in psychology that she might enjoy, and told her where she could get them if she wanted. I gave a brief enthusiastic description of each. I told her that they wouldn't take long to read and if she wanted to talk after she completed a book, she was welcome to come back and discuss it. Jana commented that she had to go to the bookstore that day and that Elaine could join her. They left.

> COMMENTS: The encouraging person must listen very attentively. A small interest was expressed in psychology; it had to be kept alive. The brief discussion held concerning the field of psychology was for two purposes: (1) to show her I was taking seriously what she was telling me; and (2) to give her more of a picture or idea of what psychology is all about.
>
> My comments regarding her difficult situation made clear to Elaine that she was being taken at face value and was understood. When I mentioned that the books wouldn't take long to read, I was indicating a belief in her ability (*I have confidence in you*). Finally, she was invited back if she wanted to talk more. This conveyed the idea that someone had the time for her—and that she was *worth* the time.

Second Interview

About a week later Elaine stopped by the office with two books in her hand, one of which I had recommended and the other Harris' *I'm OK, You're OK*.[1] I invited her in. She said she had completely read the first book and was just starting to

[1] Thomas A. Harris, *I'm OK, You're OK* (New York: Harper & Row, 1969).

read *I'm OK, You're OK*. She expressed concern that this book might be a little too difficult for her. Also she revealed that she had never been a good reader. She couldn't recall ever having finished a book in her life. I said that it was not unusual for people to have no interest in reading for years, but then to read a good book and be "turned on." I added that one thing I was sure of was that if people don't try, they'll never find that interest in reading. She had additional questions about some of the content of the first book. Her questions seemed to focus on the importance of early childhood. We talked briefly about some psychoanalysts' ideas of early childhood versus some behaviorists' ideas. I wrote a few names of popular books and their authors for her, in case she wanted to do some additional reading. She left the office with a slight spring in her step.

COMMENTS: In a sense, Elaine didn't appear to be the same person as in the first discussion. She looked different and had more of a curiosity about life. Her arrival without an appointment could have several possible meanings: (1) Did she fear she would have been rejected if she had tried to schedule an appointment? (2) Did she decide to come in spontaneously?

Another possible identity emerged from her revelation that she never had been good at reading. This, in a sense, showed some progress. She was revealing herself and a weakness. Was this, in a small way, reflecting a self-image of stupidity? It would not have been appropriate to respond by brushing off the problem. This was very real for her, and it was important for me as an encourager to implement the idea that you can't sweep "inner reality" under the rug. I tried to help her see that this problem wasn't unusual. I used enthusiasm and tried to motivate her further by the suggestion that one doesn't grow without effort. It was at this interview that Elaine showed signs of starting to develop a desire to search for meaning. I wondered how she had managed to "find time" to read, but I felt it too early to delve into this point. Could it be that a goal or purpose in life gave her more energies?

Third Interview

A little over two weeks later, Elaine called for an appointment. I was surprised to see her name in my appointment book with the addition "admissions interview." I thought this must be in error. When she arrived she had with her a spring term schedule of classes. She spoke briefly of having read *Walden Two*[2] by Skinner and Ginott's *Between Parent and Child.*[3] She expressed a concern about how she was bringing up her children. Then she told me that she had decided that she'd like to attend college on a part-time basis. But, she added, there were problems. Frankly, she felt that her high school grades would keep her out; besides, she had been away from school a number of years and this might affect her performance even if she was admitted. I explained to her the college's "open-door" policy and she was elated. It was hard for me to imagine that she was the same person I had met three short weeks before. Her second concern could only be answered by time, but I let her know that I believed that if she worked as hard on her course as she had over the last three weeks, she would make it with flying colors. I asked her how her husband felt about her going to school and she replied with some amusement, "He thinks I'm crazy." She asked if she could buy the textbook today (two weeks before classes started), and I referred her to the bookstore.

COMMENTS: In this interview, it was pretty obvious that life was starting to take on positive meaning for Elaine. From the routine "rut" in which she had lived,

[2]B. F. Skinner, *Walden Two* (New York: Macmillan Publishing Co., Inc., 1960).
[3]Haim Ginnott, *Between Parent and Child* (New York: Avon, 1965).

she was beginning to see perceptual alternatives—other ways of looking at her life. Previously she had put a great negative sign on life. Now she was changing that. Her mind was occupied with positive things and she was showing signs of excitement about the future. Her concern about college admission was real, but fortunately a flexible policy allowed her to proceed with her goal. During this interview she even seemed more intelligent and alert than before. Somehow I felt that even her housework and her family relations might be improving. This was verified later by her friend Jana.

Two years later, Elaine graduated and received her Associate's Degree in Liberal Arts. Currently studying for her Bachelor's Degree, she is also involved with two local volunteer groups. She describes her family relationships as improved and appears to have experienced many positive new identities. Elaine is now in the process of "encouraging" her husband to attend college. She is a happy, whole, "turned-on" person.

Bibliography

ADLER, A., *Understanding Human Nature.* New York: Greenberg Publishers, 1927.
———, *Social Interest.* New York: Putnam, 1939.

ALBERTI, ROBERT E., and MICHAEL L. EMMONS, *Your Perfect Right.* San Luis, Obispo: Blake Printing, 1970.

ANSBACHER, H., and ROWENA ANSBACHER, *The Individual Psychology of Alfred Adler.* New York: Basic Books, Inc., 1956.

AXLINE, VIRGINIA M., *Dibs: In Search of Self.* Boston: Houghton Mifflin, 1964.

CARLSMITH, J. M., and E. ARONSON, "Some Hedonic Consequences of the Confirmation and Disconfirmation of Expectancies," *Journal of Abnormal and Social Psychology* 66, no. 2 (1963), 151–156.

DINKMEYER, DON, and RUDOLF DREIKURS, *Encouraging Children to Learn: The Encouragement Process.* Englewood Cliffs, N.J.: Prentice-Hall, 1963.

DINKMEYER, DON, and GARY MCKAY, *Parent's Handbook: Systematic Training for Effective Parenting*. Circle Pines, Minn.: American Guidance Service, 1976.

DREIKURS, RUDOLF, *Coping with Children's Misbehavior*. New York: Hawthorne Books, 1972.

DREIKURS, RUDOLF, and LAUREN GRAY, *A New Approach to Discipline: Logical Consequences*. New York: Hawthorne Books, 1968.

ELLIS, ALBERT, *Humanistic Psychotherapy*. New York: McGraw-Hill, 1973.

————, *Reason and Emotion in Psychotherapy*. Secaucus, N.J.: Lyle Stuart, 1962.

ELLIS, ALBERT, and ROBERT A. HARPER, *A Guide to Rational Living*. Englewood Cliffs, N.J.: Prentice-Hall, 1961.

FESTINGER, L., "A Theory of Social Comparison Processes," *Human Relations*, 7 (1954), 69, 117–140.

GINOTT, HAIM, *Between Parent and Child*. New York: Avon Books, 1965.

GLASSER, WILLIAM, *Reality Therapy*. New York: Harper & Row, 1975.

HAMACHECK, DON E., *Human Dynamics in Psychology and Education*. Boston: Allyn & Bacon, 1968.

MASLOW, ABRAHAM, *Motivation and Personality*. New York: Harper & Row, 1954.

————, *The Farther Reaches of Human Nature*. New York: Viking Press, 1971.

PERLS, F., *Gestalt Therapy Verbatim*. Moab, Utah: The Real People Press, 1969.

PURKEY, WILLIAM W., *The Self Concept in School Achievement*. Englewood Cliffs, N.J.: Prentice-Hall, 1971.

REICHMAN, FREIDA FROMM, *Principles of Intensive Psychotherapy*. Chicago: University of Chicago Press, 1950.

ROGERS, CARL R., *On Becoming A Person*. Boston: Houghton Mifflin, 1961.

ROSENTHAL, ROBERT, and LENORE JACOBSEN, *Pygmalion in the Classroom*. New York: Holt, Rinehart and Winston, 1968.

SCHACHTER, S., *The Psychology of Affiliation*. Stanford, Calif.: Stanford University Press, 1959.

SKINNER, B. F., *About Behaviorism*. New York: Knopf, 1973.

STANDAL, STANLEY, "The Need for Positive Regard: A Contribution to Client-Centered Theory," unpublished Ph. D. thesis, University of Chicago, 1954.

Index